$300k @ 26

By Josh Jones
Foreword by Ben Gay III

Happy About

20660 Stevens Creek Blvd., Suite 210
Cupertino, CA 95014

Published by Happy About®
20660 Stevens Creek Blvd., Suite 210, Cupertino, CA 95014
http://happyabout.com

First Printing: September 2019
Paperback ISBN: 978-1-60005-281-1 1-60005-281-9
eBook ISBN: 978-1-60005-282-8 1-60005-282-7
Place of Publication: Silicon Valley, California, USA
Paperback Library of Congress Number: 2019908052

Trademarks

All terms mentioned in this book that are known to be trademarks or service marks have been appropriately capitalized. Neither THiNKaha, nor any of its imprints, can attest to the accuracy of this information. Use of a term in this book should not be regarded as affecting the validity of any trademark or service mark.

Warning and Disclaimer

Every effort has been made to make this book as complete and as accurate as possible. The information provided is on an "as is" basis. The author(s), publisher, and their agents assume no responsibility for errors or omissions. Nor do they assume liability or responsibility to any person or entity with respect to any loss or damages arising from the use of information contained herein.

Dedication

For Trendy, Zaylee, Sunny, Truly, and Aubree. You five princesses make my life a fairytale.

May your future be full of hard work that leads to exceptional success and happiness.

Contents

Gratitude

Before I begin, I would like to set the tone. While visiting Denver, I attended a presentation and book signing by one of my heroes. I had faithfully watched his video blog for years and loved reading his books, and I was excited to finally meet this celebrity. I'd seen him on various interviews on national television, and I had read tons of material he had published. I admired him so much, but unfortunately, the book signing ruined that for me. When I met him in person, he came off as, how my wife would describe, an "arrogant prick who only cared about himself." What a letdown! From what I could tell, he thought he was better than everyone else. I had the book signed, but from that day on, I stopped watching and reading anything he published. I tried to jump back in on a number of occasions, but when I heard his voice, I just remembered how rude he was to me. His snobby and conceited attitude drove me crazy. He seemed to have an incurable god complex, and I wanted no part of it. He took credit for everything he had predicted in the financial markets and for all his business's success. He didn't once acknowledge that maybe, *just* maybe, there was someone else in his life, past or present, who had helped him be successful. I, in no way, want to be like that gentleman.

On that note, I'd like to express to you, my dear reader, that I have so much gratitude for the people who have led me to my current state. I'm so incredibly happy. I have a beautiful wife and four incredible daughters. I have the freedom and ability to live where I want and to provide my family with the necessities of life. We want for nothing. I have had mentors and heroes and family and friends who have picked me up and pushed me forward. As I reflect on my life, it's tough to take credit for any of my achievements because I have been shaped and molded by literally thousands of inspiring and influential individuals. Although their impact may have seemed small, it has made a lasting difference in my life.

In addition to the influence of these mentors, I was also raised in a God-fearing and God-loving home, which has greatly impacted my life. Throughout this book, you'll only notice a handful of references to the role spirituality has played in my life, but I would like to acknowledge that I believe I am nothing without the strength my divine Creator has given me. I have felt inspired and sustained by a power greater than myself, as I have written many of these chapters. Throughout my life, I have felt guided and protected by an all-powerful Being. Regardless if you are of the same opinion, I would like you to know that

I sincerely believe that any wisdom shared within these pages stems from the source of all light and truth.

Lastly, I am grateful to you for taking your valuable time to read this book. I hope that as you apply these principles, you will experience a desire to change and improve your life. I want you to act—not just read. If your intention is to read only, don't waste your time. As you act and change, though, never forget to acknowledge and thank the thousands of people who have helped you succeed.

Foreword

Dear Reader,

I still remember the thrill of my first sale. I was selling boxes of Krispy Kreme doughnuts for a fundraiser. I set out with a determination to knock doors in order to win the grand prize, a brand-new, bright red bicycle. Before going out, my father taught me the best way to knock on a door.

In the south, everyone has a screen door. He told me after knocking on the door, I needed to step back far enough so that the homeowner had to open their screen door to see who was there. I would then hand them the box of doughnuts and say, "It's Krispy Kreme doughnuts time!"

On the first sale, I knocked on the door, handed the woman the box of donuts, and said my line. The woman went back inside her house, got her purse, came right back out, and paid me! I thought, "Oh this is nice!" And just like that, I was hooked on selling! That first experience later helped me with other childhood business endeavors and all of my sales interactions for years to come.

Throughout the years, I picked up many different titles: President, CEO, Executive Consultant, Coach, Speaker, Sales Trainer, and Author. However, I am first and foremost a salesman. I absolutely love it. It's the backbone of everything I have accomplished!

When I was twenty-two, I was full of myself, but I had nothing going for me at all except a wife who would have liked to have her nursing school tuition paid. One day, I saw an ad in the *Atlanta Journal Constitution* that said something like, "If you know anything about marketing plans and want to make more money, dial this number." Well, I didn't even know what a marketing plan was, but I knew I needed to make more money! I was making just $100/week at the time. Even adjusted for inflation from then to now, that was bad!

But it turns out I was about to step onto a rocket ship of an opportunity . . . right alongside some of the greatest sales professionals ever known! I went to a telephone booth, called the phone number from the ad, and began to interview the gentleman on the other end of the line. I was trying to decide if I would grace him with my presence at an interview. Seriously.

Just as I was warming up the person on the other end of the line, he abruptly stated, "Mr. Gay, I'm not the person standing in a phone booth answering want ads." He then asked where I was. I told him, and he said, "Good, you're near my office." He gave me the address and said, "Be standing in front of my desk in 10 minutes, or don't ever call this number again!" and he hung up. I yelled for my friend and future business partner, Jimmy Rucker, to pull up the car. Then, like Batman and Robin, we rushed to the address I was given. We arrived with a minute or two to spare, and I sat down by a curly-haired guy seated in the waiting room.

I said, "Hi, my name is Ben Gay, what's yours?"

He replied with a chuckle, "Ben Gay?!" Then he proceeded into all of the possible jokes you can make to a person named Ben Gay.

When he finished, I asked again, "And what's your name?"

He said, "Zig Ziglar."

I said, "With a name like 'Zig Ziglar,' you're making fun of 'Ben Gay?' You've got to be kidding me!"

I had never heard of him, and neither had anyone else—yet. At that time, he was just a cookware salesman from Columbia, South Carolina.

Before I left the office that day, Bill Dempsey, the gentleman on the phone who hired me, gave me an old scratched-up vinyl record of *The Strangest Secret* by Earl Nightingale and an old beat-up copy of *Think and Grow Rich* by Dr. Napoleon Hill, both of which I still have to this day. He said, "Listen to this record and read this book. You're going to need them."

I listened to the record and read the book, but I didn't do well at first because I didn't listen to instructions and/or learn the script. I thought personality alone would carry me along. As I got serious and learned what I needed to learn to succeed, that all started to change. I figured out if you come in early, stay late, work on weekends, memorize the presentation, and learn the product backwards and forwards, then you'll be able to spend your day talking to qualified prospects, and you'll get your sales. Success began to flow!

Little did I know when we first met, Zig and I would soon be competing head-to-head in a year-long competition where the first-place prize was a "mystery prize" and the second-place prize was a Rolls-Royce. Zig celebrated his victory early, while I was still out selling through the very last night. I won by only two sales that had been made in the final hours of the competition. As the winner of the "mystery prize," I was named president of the whole company, which soon became the largest MLM/direct sales organization in the world at the time!

Years later, I was sitting down to dinner in my home in California with Earl Nightingale and Dr. Hill, and I told them that same story. They asked me if their book and record helped me. To which I replied, "Well, you're sitting in a 7,000-square-foot home, and you both work for me . . . so yeah, your material helped a lot! Minus your book, Doctor Hill, and your record, Earl, I'm not sure we'd all be sitting here together tonight."

The world needs sales success stories to be shared. *$300K @ 26* is one such story. I believe it will inspire thousands to take the leap into the sales field, to keep knocking doors, to keep facing rejection, to fanatically learn the scripts, and ultimately, to achieve unimaginable success!

Looking at Josh is like looking into a time machine, except my hair wasn't quite as dark. Josh is about the age I was when I just started getting some traction. I get a thrill out of it because I know what's to come. There will be some ups and downs, but I know what's ahead of him, and it's going to be one amazing ride! There are people who wouldn't believe this kind of success is possible from knocking on doors. This book is your proof. Here's the story.

The advice I have for everyone reading this book: Get serious sooner! Read this entire book and internalize what you read. Josh is poised to be one of the Napoleon Hills, Earl Nightingales, or Zig Ziglars of today. As those authors transformed my life, these words can inspire the same thrilling results that I, too, experienced at a very young age.

All the best!

Ben Gay III
Editor/Author/Publisher
"The Closers" Series

The Income Percentile Curve by Age

As I write this, I'm twenty-six years old. In 2016, I earned approximately $300,000. Toward the end of that year, I was going through my finances preparing to pay taxes, and I wondered how I might rank compared to other twenty-six-year-olds. With sudden curiosity, I pulled up Google and typed in "income percentile by age." The first result was a personal finance site called DQYDJ, or Don't Quit Your Day Job. For their site, they created an easy-to-use tool where you can plug in your age and income, and it will automatically generate a graph showing an income percentile distribution according to your age. You can see how you rank at this site: https://dqydj.com/income-percentile-by-age-calculator.

I took the same data they used from the Annual Social and Economic Supplement (ASEC) and recreated that same chart I saw. The difference is the top of the chart on DQYDJ's website stopped just over $150,000.

The following chart is completely fascinating, almost mesmerizing:

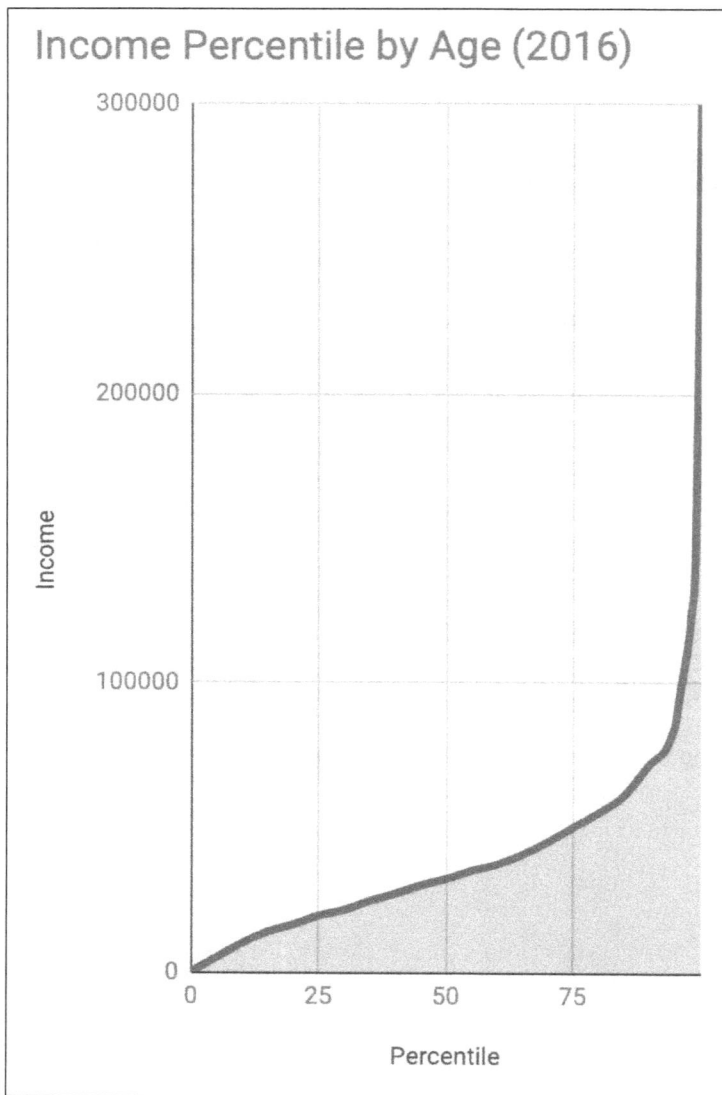

Income Percentile by Age (2016)

Image 1: Income Calculator

Let's talk about this graph for a bit. The 99th percentile starts at $153,169—my income from last year basically doubles that amount! Right around the $80,000 mark is where the income rate curves vertically for my age group. I'm writing this book because as I was staring at this graph, completely captivated, I realized that I was literally off the charts. I had the sudden realization that I've been extremely blessed throughout my life and career, and I wanted to share what it took to get to this point. Thanks to lasting guidance from mentors and life-shaping experiences, I've achieved my current financial status, as well as success in other areas of my life. Income is simply a measurable indicator of how truly fortunate I've been in my life thus far.

Assuming my high school graduating class, which consisted of about 100 people, perfectly matched these statistics, my current income would triple the income of the fifth highest earner of my entire graduating class! How did that happen?!

This year, my wife and I bought our first home. My mortgage payment, including taxes and other fees is $2,600, but I pay $3,000 to pay it off quicker. We own both of our cars 100 percent. Additionally, I paid $10,000 cash for a white baby grand piano and didn't even blink. When my wife gave birth to our third daughter, we also paid cash for that (although, it was a homebirth, so it cost a fraction of what a hospital birth costs). I also just dropped $4,400 on LASIK, and I've donated about $30,000 to my church this year. Despite these expenses, I have roughly $100,000 in my bank accounts, $20,000 in stocks, and $15,000 in miscellaneous investments. To top that off, my company owes me about $30,000 that will be paid out over the next month. My net worth is roughly $150,000–$200,000. When you compare that with the statistics we see today, which show that most people have next to nothing saved, these figures are totally unheard of, especially for a twenty-six-year-old!

How did I get here? That's the idea we're going to explore throughout this book. Twenty-six years old, $300k income. The median yearly income for that age group is $32,000, and here I am, making nearly ten times the amount the average person my age makes! Is there something wrong with Millennials? Is the economy bad? Am I just super lucky?

This book is intended for anyone who wants to be off-the-charts successful, quicker than anyone else their age. This is for teenagers looking for guidance, wondering if college is right for them or not. This is for college students looking for summer internships or jobs. This is for parents and grandparents looking for a model of growth and development for their children. This is for anyone trying to sell a product or service, wondering if there really is a pot of gold at the end of the sales rainbow. This is for the underpaid, underachieving, underworked individual living below their potential. If you think you've arrived at the point where you can't learn anything, then this isn't for you. Socrates said, "I am the wisest man alive, for I know one thing, and that is that I know nothing."

Furthermore, I want this experience documented for my children. Whatever field, hobby, sport, career, or other pursuit they embark in, I want them to strive to be exceptional. I want them to be off the charts in the ninety-ninth percentile— beyond where the curve goes vertical. I want to provide them and my readers with a roadmap for exceptional success. I'm not talking about average success: this isn't the $32k-per-year book, this is the multiple-hundreds-of-thousands-of-dollars-per-year book. I'm a huge believer that it's possible to observe and learn from the elite and then replicate exactly what led to their success. Much, if not all, of what I share can be duplicated. One of my mentors will earn significantly more than what I'll earn this year, and he's only a year older than I am. When we first met, I tried to copy his actions so intensely that I now even have the same contagious laugh. When he writes a book, I'll be first in line to buy it! There's always room for growth and improvement. There's always someone out there from whom, if you humble yourself, you can learn.

The levels of success that I've achieved and the path I've taken to get here aren't exclusive to me. Everything I've done can be done by any human being with an IQ over 70. Get tested—chances are that if you're reading this book, you make the cut. More importantly, I think your heart and determination to succeed, with a little guidance, are what will ultimately help you achieve your dreams.

This book is my roadmap; yours may be very different, but I promise that as you read this and follow your own unique passions, you'll see a plethora of parallels and applications to your life. In the scientific world, there are universal formulas. If you combine certain elements and conditions together, you get certain results. We live in a world governed by these laws of science. Income has become a chemical reaction to me; like mixing vinegar and baking soda, I know that certain actions will always yield similar results. I'm going to share with you the tried-and-true formulas of success that I've learned, applied, and found to be the most impactful and critical for big results.

I'm not a multimillionaire or a billionaire; I *am* on the path to having an extremely successful life, though. I want to walk you through the path that got me to where I am today, and share with you the best philosophies that I've adopted along the way. If what I write changes one person's life, and they achieve a similar level of success, it was worth my time to write this book. Maybe that person is you.

1 Defining Success

Worthy Goal or Ideal

Earl Nightingale said it best, "Success is the progressive realization of a worthy goal or ideal." Money is a fruit of success, but making money doesn't necessarily mean you're successful.

Is a drug dealer successful? Is their goal of selling drugs worthy? I don't believe so. What is the end result for their customers? A drug dealer helps foster the mental, emotional, financial, and spiritual decay, and often, the death of their customers. Drugs create an ever-increasing dependence just for the user to feel normal. Addicts will often spend all their money and then turn to violence and stealing just to get another fix. Some sacrifice their family relationships, spend years in rehab, live in and out of prison, and ultimately become burdens to society. What is the end result for these customers? Destruction. Do drug dealers have enough faith in their own product to use it themselves? Is it a worthy goal to make a living by making or selling illicit drugs? Not a chance.

That's an extreme case, but think about your job: what is the end result for the customer? Would you like to be your own customer?

Now, let's compare that example with the opportunity I chose to make my career. I work in direct sales for a solar energy company. This year, I personally helped over 100 homeowners reduce or eliminate their dependence on fossil fuels for their electricity. This change in power consumption will last for twenty to thirty years. Their average electric savings rate was 35 percent. This translates to saving an average of $600/year. That savings is expected to grow because we give customers a protected rate, meaning their prices increase at a much slower pace than their current utility companies'. Let's assume, though, that savings doesn't grow. $600 x 100 = $60,000/year that my new customers will save. Twenty years down the road, the total savings grows to $1.2 million. My customers spent nothing extra out of their pockets to collectively save over a million dollars! When you add the rate protection, that savings will be many times larger.

I sleep so well at night knowing that I'm working for a noble cause; I'm helping my neighbors and friends save money! Success is not success unless it's coupled with inner peace, which comes from progressing toward a worthy goal or ideal.

Expanding Your Sphere of Influence

Another element of success is the footprint you leave. How big is your impact on the lives of others?

According to Wikipedia, "Van Gogh was unsuccessful during his lifetime, and was considered a madman and a failure. He became famous after his suicide." Now, he is "among the most famous and influential figures in the history of Western art."[1]

I don't want to be like Van Gogh; I want to make the world a better place while I'm still alive. I want to spread a positive influence to hundreds and thousands—and ultimately, millions or even billions—of individuals. How big is your sphere of influence? How will your influence determine the success of others? Are you using that influence for good? Would people say they are better off after having met and learned from you?

I see many aspects of life as one big multilevel marketing pyramid. The way to really expand your influence is to teach, train, and develop other people so they can, in turn, be influential. First of all, before anyone will ever listen to you, you have to learn for yourself that you're worth more than $10/hour. You have to learn to multiply your income and value by ten. Be worth $100/hour. How do you do that? In Chapter 3, I talk about what it felt like when I almost sold my soul to learn how to multiply my value. It's not easy at all; that jump in income and mentality is super dramatic. Jumping from $10/hour to $20/hour is nothing

---

[1]"Vincent van Gogh," Wikipedia, Wikimedia Foundation, last modified 16 October 2017, 15:26, https://en.wikipedia.org/wiki/Vincent_van_Gogh.

super impressive. In order to get other people excited to follow you, you have to experience an exponential increase in your true value. No one gets pumped up to follow a leader who lives an average life making average money. Alexander the Great was an over-the-top, incredible leader who influenced entire nations. If he hadn't been an exceptional leader, his life would have been a much different narrative. He might have been called Alexander the Average instead, and you wouldn't even recognize his name now. We wouldn't even know about him if he hadn't first focused on his personal development and learned from the philosopher Aristotle. That mentorship taught him how to be one of the most influential rulers of all time. In Chapters 5 and 6, I explore the mentorship I've received and the most effective ways I've learned and developed myself.

Continuing to the next step in expanding your influence, after you've become exceptional, teach others to be exceptional. Help them open their mind and see the possibilities. Then, help them see their potential. Repeat. Focus, then, on a core group of students who are eager to share the knowledge with others. Your influence will multiply as those five or ten people share your wisdom with another five or ten people and so on. The results of your teaching will compound and expand faster than you can track. Your positive influence ultimately becomes immeasurable. You'll learn more about exponential growth in Chapters 11 and 15.

One example of essentially unlimited impact is writing a book. I'm so excited to write and publish this book because this is a way to expand my influence and to share the wealth of knowledge that I've received from so many different influential heroes and heroines in my life. I'm so grateful for those people that as a tribute and token of that gratitude for their mentorship, I want to spread their influence even further. I can't spend good quality time with even hundreds of people, let alone thousands, but through a book, I can record my thoughts and the wisdom I've gained and therefore, have the potential to reach and change billions of lives.

These expansions of our impact on the world start with an expansion of character and ambition in ourselves. I can only help someone come to *my* own level of achievement and understanding. For this reason, it's important to first become successful, then share that success with the world. Many people in leadership roles have a flawed mentality: they try to encourage and motivate others by telling them what to do rather than *showing* them what to do. I've learned over the years that 100 percent of the time, the most successful leaders *lead from the front*. As you do this, your circle of influence expands, and the success you enjoy personally is magnified by fostering the success of others. I don't think success is true success unless it's shared with the world. A hermit who lives in a cave with a chest of gold coins and talks to no one is not successful, no matter how much gold he has.

I was so incredibly blessed to make so much money this past year; however, in my eyes, my success was not in earning the money. Money was a byproduct. My success was in my influence, in pushing people to new levels of achievement, shaping new paradigms, and improving the quality of life of those around me.

Zig Ziglar sums up this notion best with this declaration: "You can have everything in life you want, if you will just help enough other people get what they want."[2] The way I see it, I successfully expanded a positive influence better than 99 percent of people my age; therefore, I was compensated financially better than that 99 percent.

The Outdoor Code

I was a Boy Scout growing up. Thanks to the bribery of my dad to earn my driver's license and the diligence of my mother chauffeuring and prodding me in the right direction, I achieved the highest rank and became an Eagle Scout. Throughout the eight years that I spent working toward that award, there was one thing that stuck with me more than anything else: the Outdoor Code. The Outdoor Code goes hand in hand with the principles of Tread Lightly and Leave No Trace. These are ethical values of the Boy Scouts, considered to be more than just mottos or slogans, and are revered by many as a way of life. They teach that whether you're hiking, camping, fishing, or just living your daily life in your own home, you should always strive to leave your surroundings better than you found them.

My greatest takeaway from that lesson is a sense of responsibility for the world. We should constantly try to make the environment, our friends, family members, neighbors, coworkers, and even our pizza delivery person better than how we found them. What if everyone in the world adopted this principle as a way of life? There wouldn't be an ISIS, and there wouldn't be world wars and holocausts. There would be no need for atomic bombs or aircraft carriers. Hate crimes and racism would come to an end, and we wouldn't always be looking over our shoulder wondering who's going to try to harm or take advantage of us.

Success, in my opinion, is adopting this mentality and then spreading it. Global change is sparked by individuals who collectively rise up and vote by their choices and their consumption habits. If you want to vote against GMOs, then buy and support organic farming. If you want to vote against coal, go solar. If you want to vote against solar, buy coal. If you're pro free trade and outsourcing, then buy foreign automobiles. The free market and our consumption choices make a huge impact on the future. The will of the people is made manifest by our actions. Towns degrade and turn to slums if everyone neglects their property and litters without shame or guilt. Civilizations, likewise, crumble as the morals of the people degrade.

---

[2]Dan Western, "34 Best Zig Ziglar Quotes on Leadership," Wealthy Gorilla, https://wealthygorilla.com/28-best-zig-ziglar-quotes-leadership/.

Any interaction with another human being should include the thought, "Am I leaving this person better off than how I found them?" The parable of the Good Samaritan from the Bible exemplifies this trait. The question posed to Jesus that prompted this parable was: "What shall I do to inherit eternal life?" The concept of eternal life is the ultimate goal and aspiration in Christianity. I'm sure everyone present was listening and paying diligent attention to every word: "And he answering said, 'Thou shalt love the Lord thy God with all thy heart, and with all thy soul, and with all thy strength, and with all thy mind; and thy neighbour as thyself.'"[3]

The follow-up question was then asked, "And who is my neighbour?"[4] Jesus replied with the following:

> And Jesus answering said, "A certain *man* went down from Jerusalem to Jericho, and fell among thieves, which stripped him of his raiment, and wounded *him,* and departed, leaving *him* half dead. And by chance there came down a certain priest that way: and when he saw him, he passed by on the other side. And likewise a Levite, when he was at the place, came and looked *on him,* and passed by on the other side. But a certain Samaritan, as he journeyed, came where he was: and when he saw him, he had compassion *on him,* and went to *him,* and bound up his wounds, pouring in oil and wine, and set him on his own beast, and brought him to an inn, and took care of him. And on the morrow when he departed, he took out two pence, and gave *them* to the host, and said unto him, 'Take care of him; and whatsoever thou spendest more, when I come again, I will repay thee.' Which now of these three, thinkest thou, was neighbour unto him that fell among the thieves?" And he said, "He that shewed mercy on him." Then said Jesus unto him, "Go, and do thou likewise."[5]

The Good Samaritan left his neighbor better than how he found him. He went out of his way to make life better for this wounded and beaten man he didn't even know. He dressed the wounds, sacrificed his own vehicle, and walked instead, and then he paid for this stranger to be cared for when he couldn't be there. Were either the priest or the Levite successful? Certainly not. Love your neighbor as yourself; leave them better than how you found them. Leave the sidewalks, parks, shopping carts, bathroom sinks, toilet seats, hiking trails, campsites, rivers, lakes, beaches, and most importantly, the people you interact with all better than you found them. When that simple Boy Scout ethical code is adopted by mankind, the world will know peace.

---

[3] Luke 10:27 KJV
[4] Luke 10:29
[5] Luke 10:30–37

2 You Must Learn to Sell!

Redefining Sales

Have you ever watched *Shark Tank*? *Shark Tank* is an incredible TV show on ABC where a panel of five or six millionaire and billionaire investors known as the "sharks" have on-screen negotiations to buy equity in small businesses. In just about every episode, it seems like someone comes in with an awesome idea that intrigues the investors, but then they get down to the nitty gritty numbers, and the businesses' appeal diminishes. The sharks' favorite question to ask is, "What are your sales?" When one of the small business owners responds with a low sales number, immediately all the sharks take a huge step back, and their interest in investing in the product or business typically goes away.

On the flip side, my man, Mr. Mark Cuban, gets giddy when someone says they've been hustling, selling their product door-to-door. His eyes light up and you can almost see his ears literally perk up in excitement. If the sharks hear a product or business idea that seems kind of boring, *but* the sales are awesome, there's usually someone who wants a piece of it.

I recently had a conversation with a friend who is a couple of years into developing his own product. He's invested tens of thousands of dollars and hundreds of thousands of dollars' worth of time; however, he only has a few thousand dollars in sales. This friend unfortunately claims to "suck at sales." Sadly, because of that self-imposed constraint, he relies on others to drive his product into the hands of the consumer. Due to this dependence, his sales are next to non-existent, *but* he has what I firmly believe to be an amazing product. Your ability to sell is the asymptote of your business; the limit of your sales volume is the limit to your business's growth. No sales = No business. No sales means you only have a business concept. No sales means you have an *unproven* business concept. As a scientist, I've approached business and sales using the well-known scientific method. I remember learning about it in preparation for the junior high science fair; little did I realize, it would one day apply to business.

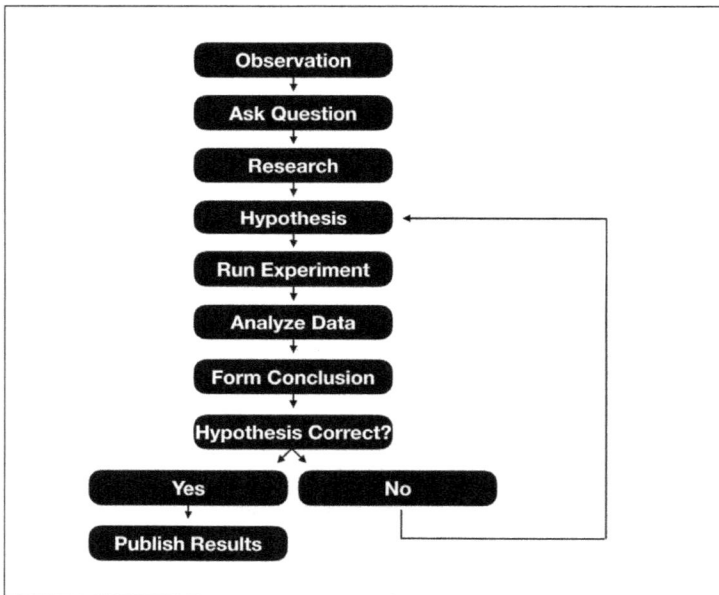

Image 2: The Scientific Method

When starting and running a business, you absolutely have to go through this process. Ask a question; find out what people want and more importantly, what they need. Then research to figure out the best way to meet those needs as you develop a business plan that becomes the scientific equivalent of your hypothesis. Finally, you get to perform the experiment. In the scientific method, the experiment is the highlight of the project or investigation. It's the part where you get to find out if your idea was right or wrong. Sales is the experiment; success or failure in sales either supports or disproves the accuracy of your hypothesis. If your experiment fails, then you have to go back a few steps and change your hypothesis and potentially squash the idea altogether. Likewise, if you or someone else can't sell your product and make a profit, then it's back to the drawing board.

Whether it's your business, your product, or even your*self*, you have to learn to sell and be an expert at it. Before you skip over this notion and say, "I'm not good at sales," or, "I suck at sales," let me attempt to change your perspective. People often equate dishonesty, pushiness, flamboyance, selfishness, and greed with sales. Have you ever gone furniture shopping and almost bought a big-ticket item but then at the last minute, changed your mind because you realized it was never what you were actually looking for? Try it sometime. The stereotypical salesman's charm will slowly disappear as they lose the sale, along with their pleasant nature. That very situation happened to me not too long ago. My wife and I were trying to furnish our new home, and we had been shopping all morning. Lunchtime came and went and we were starving. We were overwhelmed and ready to take a break, but we felt like we couldn't leave that miserable Ashley's Furniture store until we bought something. Two salespeople double-teamed us, and we felt so uncomfortable. Nature tends to take over in these situations, resulting in the defense mechanism options of fight, flight, or freeze. You can either be rude and fight with the salesperson, run away in a frenzied panic (which, for some reason, doesn't seem socially acceptable), or sit pensively, pretending to be indecisive, saying nothing at all until the store closes or the sales rep loses interest in you and finds a new victim. Sound familiar? No one likes being on either side of any of those interactions! In the end, my wife doesn't like confrontation, and we were too exhausted to run, so we ended up defaulting to the third defense mechanism, only further delaying our lunch.

The sales process doesn't have to be like that! Let's change your definition of sales. The most important principle of sales to understand is *agency*. As humans, we are proactive, not reactive. No one can or should try to force anyone to buy something. People don't *sell* to people, people *buy* from other people. My college sales professor said it best:

Sales = Helping People Buy

This shift in definition should help you see that working in sales means selflessly serving—not selfishly pushing. Permission is required for a transaction to occur. In order to receive permission, there must first be understanding. Your role as a sales professional should shift from coercion to instruction. Sales gives you the benefit of getting to teach every day without having to live on a teacher's salary. How many teachers with a four-year degree make over six figures? How many teachers even have the potential to make more than $100K? As your definition of sales evolves from pushing to educating and you gain the sincere desire to help others, I guarantee that you'll see a massive increase in your sales performance and ultimately, your income.

There are a few chapters in this book dedicated to helping increase sales performance. In those chapters, I'll explain how I personally reached a high level of competence, and I'll share the techniques and secrets that have made me more successful than I ever thought I would be at this age. However, this new definition of sales must first be internalized before those skills can be implemented. This concept of becoming an educator with the mission of helping others is what has really made the biggest difference for me. I've spent years working to become, what many would consider, an expert salesman. My customers often comment on my sales skills, but they are infinitely more impressed with my character. Because I've done my best to adopt the formula that Sales = Helping People Buy, I've quickly earned the trust of customers. It's apparent that I respectfully want to help them understand so that they can *choose* to buy. Once this definition of sales is ingrained, you will undoubtedly see similar results.

Unlimited Upside

About a year ago, I was curious about what type of job I would do if I left sales. I spent a good hour or two looking through job listings to see what was available. I can honestly say that I wasn't impressed by any of the choices. Anything really fun wouldn't pay the bills or didn't exist, and anything making a decent wage was boring and capped by an hourly rate or a salary. There are only twenty-four hours in a day; that means my maximum earnings would be predetermined by those hours. That is one factor that is completely beyond my control—time is limited, and consequently, so is your pay. That feeling of being powerless would drive me absolutely crazy. With my job, there are so many ways to create more income just by working smarter. I can leverage my resources to change my hourly rate to be just about as high as I want. There's a pretty impenetrable earnings ceiling on just about every job in the world, except sales. Commission is such a beautiful word. For both an employee as well as an employer, that word should be music to your ears. Here's why:

Hourly Pay = Pay based on simply showing up

Commission = Pay based on *value* added to the business

There's a massive difference in attitude when you're paid hourly vs paid commission. When employees are incentivized based on performance, productivity is maximized, hands down. It's so easy to waste time, letting your ingenuity and creativity die, when your presence is all that's required to get you a paycheck. Hourly employees don't necessarily add value to the company, equivalent to what they're paid; they can easily drain a business's time and resources. Furthermore, they aren't held to the same level of accountability as a commission worker. Here's a list of some striking differences in attitude between the two forms of pay.

Hourly	Commission
If you're hourly, how long will your lunch break be? As long as possible.	If you're commission, how long will your lunch break be? As short as possible. What's a lunch break?
What if you're hourly and finish your work early? You get paid for sitting around playing solitaire or browsing Facebook.	What if you're commission and finish your work early? It's impossible to finish early, the potential workload is never-ending. Your job is to create new business; that task never stops.
If you're hourly, why would you need to have good rapport and refine your customer service skills when talking to people? You get paid whether or not the customers are happy.	What if you're commission-based? You bend over backwards to make customers happy because if they cancel their purchase or decide not to purchase again, *you* are directly affected.
If you're hourly, you don't work outside of your allotted 9-to-5 window or whatever your schedule may be. You rarely, if ever, take work calls unless you're clocked in. Why would you? You aren't making any extra money by going above and beyond.	If you're commission, you're on call for most of your life because a customer may call with a question or a referral. Either way, you're available because your livelihood depends on how well you treat your customers.

Do you work for hourly pay? Learn to sell. Leave the shackles of your hourly prison, stretch yourself further than your comfort zone, and live up to your true potential. The model of hourly wages does not inspire urgency or creativity; it unfortunately doesn't encourage people to be their best selves.

I recommend door-to-door sales as a good start because that's where I started . . . and where I still am. I don't care how old and "experienced" you are; if I, with my lack of experience, can earn more than most doctors and lawyers at 26 by knocking doors, then imagine the success a seasoned professional could have. Door-to-door sales isn't beneath you.

It's pretty funny; quite often, people will ask me questions like, "Are you ever going to get a real job?" I also have people recommending their job to me. Someone last year told me I need to get a job as a high school teacher because apparently in Connecticut, that's a profession where I can make "incredible" money. He was talking about $80,000 a year, which would've required me going back to school and then working for decades to get my pay potential maxed out . . . no, thank you. If you're a teacher, then I'm sorry, zero offense is intended, but the sad reality is that teaching just isn't a job with much income potential. Personally, I would feel trapped and limited by uncontrollable factors. A sales profession puts the salesperson in control of their paycheck, and because of that control, I've chosen to work hard enough and smart enough to earn more than most people think is even possible. It's incredible how efficient you can become when you essentially write your paycheck every week based on the quality and quantity of your work.

I love telling my wife those stories about people suggesting new jobs for me; she just laughs and says, "Did you tell them how much you make?" I'm pretty shy about sharing how much I make, so no one really knows. When I first started writing this book, I was so excited to tell people about my new project. When you say that, for some reason, one of the first questions everyone asks is, "What's the title?" I didn't want anyone to know the name though because then they would know how successful I was. I acted almost like I was ashamed of my success. My reason for not sharing my income has been to avoid the appearance of arrogance and pride. I don't want anyone to get the impression that I think I'm somehow better than they are because I make more money than they do. I don't feel that way one bit. I feel like the playing field is equal; we have equal opportunity to succeed, *but* we have to make the correct decisions in order to come out ahead. That's a huge reason why I'm writing this, so I can share what I did to get here. A huge factor was learning to sell. It wasn't easy; in fact, it was quite miserable. I'll share some parts of that experience in the next chapter. On top of that, there will be a few chapters throughout this book that will teach you my biggest takeaways that I gleaned as a result of mastering the sales profession. I'll also teach you how to master sales or anything else you put your mind to.

My parents always told me I could accomplish anything I put my mind to. I'm going to tell you the same thing now. Maybe you didn't have the same childhood I did. Maybe you didn't have the same love and support that helped nurture my confidence and intellect. That's okay. Moving forward, the playing field is level. You're in control of your own destiny. Choose today to make the most of your life. For me, sales helped me get there. Choose what you want to do, and I'm certain that if you learn the fundamentals of sales and embrace the idea of earning according to the value that you add, you'll be on the fast track to success.

The Perfect Presentation

An integral part of sales is giving a presentation. Likewise, the purpose of just about every presentation is to encourage someone to buy your idea, point of view, or product. Your goal is for someone to see and understand your point of view and consequently adopt your attitudes, beliefs, or values. Therefore, knowing how to give a good presentation is extremely valuable in any field. Two of the most valuable courses I ever took were a beginning acting class and an introductory public speaking course. In those classes, I learned how to deliver a compelling presentation that keeps people engaged. It's important to understand that there are three main ways to give a presentation:

1. **Impromptu:** This style is when you basically make up your presentation on the fly. This requires an extraordinary amount of natural talent that I don't have. The challenges to presenting extemporaneously are that it's difficult to stay on topic, and if you're underprepared, your content can lack in quality and cohesion. This style of presenting is typically not

the best way to move a sale forward. However, it has the potential to be upbeat, fast-paced, and fun. Impromptu allows a lot of spontaneous humor and personality to shine through. These are the raw, unorganized thoughts that go from the brain to the mouth without advanced time to process them. This type of presentation can be appropriate at times— for example, when giving a toast.

2. **Memorized:** The memorized approach is exactly how it sounds. You repeat verbatim what you have written out or pre-rehearsed. In sales, there are a few risks to using this method. You have to be careful not to sound like a TV commercial or a robot. Certain human elements are often missing in the delivery of a memorized presentation. The lack of spontaneity in a rote presentation just doesn't do it for most people. Multiple times in the past, I've answered the phone thinking a telemarketer with a memorized pitch was actually a recording and, with shock, have even replied: "I thought you were a machine!" Giving a memorized speech or reading your presentation is appropriate at certain times, such as when the President of the United States delivers the State of the Union Address. When a presentation has vital information to cover or a lengthy time requirement, reading a carefully constructed speech is the way to go.

3. **Guided:** In my opinion, the best way to give a presentation merges the best of both worlds. A guided presentation utilizes extemporaneous speaking while following an *outline* that was prepared in advance. It requires significantly more thought, practice, and preparation than the other two ways. I would compare this type to the porridge that Goldilocks ended up eating. It's not too word-for-word robotic, and it's not too spur-of-the-moment superficial; it's just right. You should practice adding in deliberate hand gestures and body language, but the execution of those movements should look natural and add emphasis to points in your message. Following an outline should skillfully use cues that prompt anecdotes that expound upon points. The anecdotes are ad-libbed and different every time. These cues help give the appeal of a natural conversation, while ensuring the speaker will stay on topic. This style of communication is guided and directed toward a specific objective with pre-planned explanations and examples that strive to enhance the receptivity of your listeners. This delivery of a presentation is akin to a conversation, while still maintaining a deliberate agenda. If you want to see a great example of this style of presentation, watch Jimmy Fallon on *The Tonight Show*.

Memorization and fine-tuning of details are important, but when it comes down to it, if you lack the human element, what's to keep people from buying similar products or services online from someone else? Do they need your help if a robot will give them the same level of interaction in addition to a lower price?

What's to keep them from staying locked indoors all day with a laptop and an Amazon Prime membership? The human interaction! There are essential elements like humor and emotion that a computer just can't offer. The guided presentation is the best way to retain humanity in sales while efficiently educating your customer.

When I was learning and honing my presentation, I started by memorizing what I would say word for word. I copied one of the best sales reps in my industry. He spent hours with me, quizzing me on what I was going to say and *how* I was going to say it. He focused on refining where I was adding emphasis and where I made certain hand gestures to strengthen my points. I didn't want to miss any details so I wrote down everything he said in my notes. This whole memorization process wasn't easy. For the first six to eight months, I had a written outline with all my talking points and cues to remind me what to say. Eventually, it was condensed to be just a word or two for each point until it evolved into visual cues or slides on my iPad that my customers saw as well. These provided visual cues to jog my memory, and each picture had clearly defined and deliberate points, directing me to say everything I needed in order to push through the sales cycle. My pitch went from being a memorized presentation to being a picture-guided outline.

This process can be replicated by anyone! Why is public speaking one of people's biggest fears? One reason is that most people think a speech is supposed to go straight from their brain to their mouth. The most successful speeches, lectures, conversations, trainings, and sales appointments I've had have all been guided by an outline. This type of presentation often requires an intense amount of preparation and practice. Unless you're a rare exception, if you don't prepare enough in advance, your presentation will fail.

In the coming chapters, I will expound on specific actions and phrases that enhance my presentation and increase the likelihood that I'll achieve my purpose, which ultimately, is that someone will buy my product. In the industry, they're known as "one-liners" and "power moves." They're necessary elements to having a perfectly executed performance.

The last note on presentations I want to include is that the best, most memorable presentations are the ones that are short, sweet, and have a powerfully profound point. Presentations can easily become too intricate, detailed, and messy. The complexity is confusing and often distracts from what needs to be remembered. When a presentation is too long, you quickly lose your audience's interest. Attention spans generally range somewhere from eight seconds to twenty minutes. I recommend being on the shorter end of that range. Over twenty minutes, and you better have some kind of a break or activity to mix things up; otherwise, your audience will not get the full value of your message. Why do you think most television sitcoms are only twenty minutes long? It all has to do with making the most of an audience's attention span.

This week, as you're on the receiving end of sales pitches and any type of presentation, pay attention to see if you can spot the elements of a guided presentation. Chances are, the best ones will have a healthy combination of both spontaneity and structure. You will probably want to buy what they're selling. Learn to sell this way and your results will instantly improve.

3 Take the Path of Most Resistance

Summer Sales

At most universities, there are prerequisite courses that are especially difficult, which are designed to weed people out. As an example, organic chemistry is a prerequisite for medical school. It's one of the toughest courses required for pre-med students. If you can't pass that grueling class, then medical school will most certainly be a challenge for you. This same idea applies to my job description. Door-to-door sales is a hated profession. Anyone who has done it can attest to the misery involved. The job itself weeds out the people who aren't willing to work for the success. A result of mastering one of the world's most difficult and demanding professions is extremely high compensation. Summer sales was my prerequisite to achieving a life-changing income.

Companies looking for a rise in sales during the summer months will often hire college students on break between semesters. Everything from pest control services to outdated scriptural DVDs, knives, and cosmetics are all marketed door-to-door by companies looking for a pop in sales during the summer months. The warm weather and long days make it the perfect time to go door-to-door. Many of those companies offer commissions that end up making those kids way more money than what they've earned in their entire lives. A lot of students pay for their education using what they earn from selling during the summer, and if they're good at it, they have extra funds to buy a new truck, ATV, or in some cases, a home or rental property. These are the people in college who weren't mooching off of Mommy or Daddy and always had money to spend.

There are mixed reviews about door-to-door sales, depending on who you talk to. Those who are mentally weak cave under the pressure of working in sales and go home, complaining about how miserable it was and how they didn't make any money. Then there's that other group of people who go out and work their butts off and make more money during one summer than what most people make throughout the entire year. I was in between the two groups, which forever changed my life.

Summer sales feels like hell—as in, damnation and a lack of progress or improvement. However, the result of summer sales for me was one of the most rapid periods of personal growth that I've ever experienced. Three consecutive years of summer sales showed me who I was, where I needed to go, and how incredibly *weak* I was. Like how a muscle grows from being worked, I grew from being pushed to my limit. I still vividly remember the miserable humidity and horrible chafing in Arkansas and Louisiana. Experiences like getting chiggers while peeing in the woods and a wasp bite to the head can really shape and refine one's character.

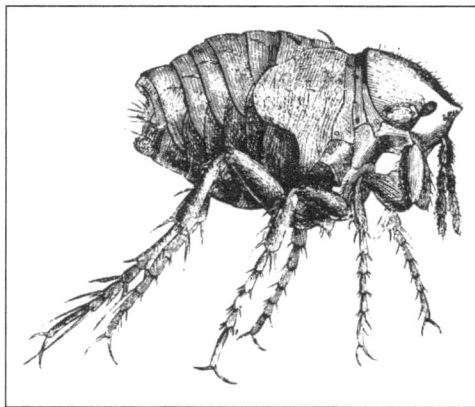
Image 3: Chigger

Having dozens of those little hellbeasts burrowing into my groin and belly was miserable. In order to get rid of them, I had to rub mayonnaise all over my body and sleep wrapped up in plastic wrap. Google "chiggers," and you'll probably never pee in the woods again either!

Most summers, I had little to no vacation in between school semesters; my schedule for the entire summer was as follows:

Monday–Friday:
- 7:30 am: Work out with my wife (if I had enough energy left to wake up for that).
- 8:00 am: Study for thirty to sixty minutes something related to sales (again, if I had enough energy left to wake up for that; for the first two summers, most of the time I would sleep in until fifteen minutes before I needed to be at my meeting because I was so exhausted from the previous day).
- 12:00 pm: Training meeting for forty-five minutes.
- 1:00 pm: Get dropped off in an assigned neighborhood and sell until 9:00 pm or later.
- 9:00–11:00 pm: Get picked up by the group driver and head home. My commute home was sometimes up to two hours. Once I got home, I would watch an episode or two of *Shark Tank* with my wife and best friend.

Saturday:
- 8:30 am: Training meeting
- 9:00/9:30am–9:00 pm: Knock on doors

Sunday:
- Three hours of church
- Rest

Rinse and repeat!

One hour of knocking on doors at 1:00 pm on a Monday feels like eight hours of almost any other job. It felt like 400-hour work weeks. I'm sure I remember one of my managers saying something like, "if you don't want to quit and go home at least once a week, then you aren't working hard enough." Unless you've been through this experience, you'll never fully know the agony, pain, heartache, and exhaustion of summer sales. Would I want to do it again? Hell NO! Would I be where I am today had I not subjected myself to this grueling experience? No way.

Taking the path of most resistance aligns perfectly with the Law of the Harvest. If you spend the time tilling the ground, planting, watering, fertilizing, weeding, pruning, and protecting your crops from pests all summer long, you'll have significantly more to harvest in the fall than if you'd sat on your rump all summer long playing video games and lollygagging. Taking the path of most resistance is the next level of the Law of the Harvest. If a crop is harder to grow, it probably is worth more. To clarify, I'm not just saying to get a job during the summer, I'm saying to get a job that beats you up! Get a job that works you, that makes you cry! I cried every single summer I sold. It was so hard, but I love that it was so extremely difficult and miserable, because now what I'm doing seems effortless, and now I'm making ten times the money.

Every college student must decide what field of study to focus on; some degrees have reputations for being extremely demanding. I chose to study chemistry in part because it's known for being a challenging major. As I'm writing this, I'm realizing that I might be a mental masochist—maybe I should be worried. Who in their right mind studies chemistry in one of the coldest towns in America during the winter, and then come summer, sells door-to-door in the muggy swamps of Louisiana? On the bright side, school was a piece of cake after a summer of selling.

I vividly remember my first week back one fall. In my organic chemistry lab, they had an icebreaker activity in which we asked our lab partner what they did for their summer vacation. My response was, "This is my vacation, I didn't get a break all summer." Let that sink in for a second: organic chemistry = vacation? Yep, summer sales *is* that rough!

The First Summer

For three years, my poison of choice was selling alarm systems. My first summer started out pretty rocky. It was going to be the first time my wife and I would be separated since we had been married. The plan was to have her drop me off at the airport, then two weeks later, she would drive from Wyoming to Arkansas to meet me and stay the rest of the summer. For whatever reason, my wife and I left pretty late to get to the Denver airport. In order to check a bag, you *have* to get to the airport forty-five minutes early; otherwise, they won't take your bag. We got there fifty minutes before my plane was scheduled to take off, so we figured we would be fine. Well, I waited in the line to check my bag for about ten minutes. My wife was already gone when they told me I couldn't check my bag. My heart sank to the curb; what was I going to do? I frantically called my wife to tell her that I needed her to come back to pick up my checked bag (which had the bulk of my necessities, including *all* my underwear). Under the pressure of a ticking clock, I dug through my suitcase looking for what I thought were the most important necessities. I then hurriedly shoved what I needed into my carry-on bag. My wife pulled up to the curb with thirty minutes to go before the terminal gates closed. I left my suitcase there once I saw her and ran inside the airport.

Have you ever seen someone sprinting through an airport in flip flops? It was probably me! I got to the security line, and it was backed up so far that it would've taken at least an hour to get through it. The line appeared to be making no progress; the situation looked more dire than the DMV! My anxiety levels spiked at this point. I proceeded to beg people in front of me to let me skip in front of them because I knew I was going to miss my flight if didn't get through sooner. I made good progress through the line until I finally got to a point where someone wouldn't let me skip in front of them. The clock was ticking, and I couldn't believe someone would tell me I couldn't move up in the line. I was so pumped for this opportunity to sell alarms that summer that I thought, "This guy is going to be the reason I miss my flight and don't fulfill my destiny." After what felt like half an eternity, I got through security and then started sprinting toward my gate. I thought I was almost there with five minutes to spare and then realized I had gone the wrong way and had no clue where I was. An airport worker told me which way to go, and I sprinted even faster than before toward my future. I got there right in the nick of time, out of breath, sweating and shaking, ready to collapse. I looked up at the sign that said Little Rock, and then heard someone announce that there was a fifteen-minute delay. People who I had passed in the security line showed up to the same gate and got in line behind me . . .

I arrived in Little Rock, and because I was broke, every single day for the next two weeks, I rewashed the one pair of underwear I was wearing when I left my suitcase at that curbside in Denver.

To start my summer, I shadowed my best friend for one day to learn the ropes, and then I was on my own. I talked to forty people a day for three days in a row, and I had no success whatsoever. I had to report in my meeting that I had "bageled"—a term for selling zero systems in a day. I was so distraught and confused. Why wasn't I selling anything and everyone else was? To make things even worse, I found out that the neighborhood I was working in had sent out a Facebook alert that someone was going around trying to scam people . . . I guess that person was me, a brand-new sales rep who didn't know how to sell. While Skyping my wife, she offered encouragement, but I could tell she was super scared to have trusted me with the prospect of a 100 percent commission job that had yielded $0 after probably close to forty hours of work.

On my fifth day of work, I finally broke through the bagel barrier! I literally begged an angry Egyptian woman to say yes. With all the passion and zeal I could muster, I told her something along the lines of, "I'm going to give you my personal cell phone number; if something happens, I'll be there for you and I'll take care of you. I know that this is the best system to protect you and your family." The desperation was felt, she had to leave, and on her way out, she told her husband, "Don't do it, honey, let's talk about it first." She left and he said, "We're doing it." The installer was on his way to throw that sucker in twenty minutes later. Getting that first sale was *so* tough, but with my newly found confidence, I got another one installed the next day. It felt euphoric to have succeeded. I was hooked on sales from that point on.

I ended my first six days of work having made about $1,000; that came out to about $16 an hour. My dad had been paying me $25 an hour back in Wyoming to help him build his house, so why was I in the humidity of Arkansas, going crazy, when I could be making more somewhere else with only physical stress rather than insane mental stress?!

At this point, I was incredibly confused. I was used to being one of the best at whatever I did: sports, school, music, learning a new language, you name it. However, with this endeavor, for some reason, I was at the bottom of the numbers board. I had expected myself to soar to the top of the company right from the beginning. I had been planning to be a doctor, something that I thought would be the toughest path I could've pursued. I quickly realized during that first traumatic week that I had found something even more difficult than medical school. Luckily, it also had a much higher potential for personal growth and income as well. I had found my "odyssey." It was a path that was tailored to my needs, that would foster my learning and self-development better than anything else I could have pursued. I had found my path of most resistance, my *"Ad Astra."* As Megara, the wife of Hercules, said in Seneca the Younger's tragedy, *Hercules Furens*: *"Non est ad astra mollis e terris via,"* meaning, "There is no easy way from the earth to the stars."[6]

There are so many terms that can be used to describe these bitter experiences of most resistance. One of them is found throughout the Bible. The authors repeatedly refer to the "refiner's fire" and its power of purification, self-actualization, and ultimately, sanctification. Isaiah 48:10 says: "Behold, I have refined you, but not as silver; I have tried you in the furnace of affliction." Yep! That pretty much sums up what I thought of Arkansas; it was my "furnace of affliction." Literally and figuratively. What a miserable place to spend July and August! It's even worse if you're away from your spouse, running on one pair of underwear, car-less, and going door-to-door, not getting on the other side of any of those doors to an air-conditioned home. The haunting flashbacks of that first week selling alarms in Arkansas still come regularly, but I love it. I love it because it was a refining and defining trial. I achieved what, for me, had been unthinkable results, unimaginable success, unbelievable happiness, and lasting fulfillment. I skipped medical school and somehow made post-medical school caliber money, as well as finding a richer meaning and purpose in life. I finally can say that I understand what Robert Frost meant when he said,

> "Two roads diverged in a wood, and I—
> I took the one less traveled by,
> And that has made all the difference."[7]

That first summer was my fork in the road. I'm not exactly sure what fortune my other path would have yielded, but I'm certain this book wouldn't have been written, and I would still be in school. I would probably still have eight or nine years of school left before being able to start my profession.

---

[6]"Ad astra (phrase)," Wikipedia, Wikimedia Foundation, last modified August 3, 2018, 20:08, https://en.wikipedia.org/wiki/Ad_astra_(phrase).
[7]Robert Frost, "The Road Not Taken," Mountain Interval, lines 23–25.

Now let's return to that first summer, five years ago. The weeks that followed that $16 an hour first week gradually improved. Here's how my weekly numbers for the rest of the summer progressed:

Week 1: 2
Week 2: 3
Week 3: 4
Week 4: 5
Week 5: 4
Week 6: 10 (my wife left to visit family on Friday of this week, and I sold five the very next day)
Week 7: 11 (This translates to about $6,000.)
Week 8: 10
Week 9: Vacation (two family reunions that were "non-negotiable" conditions from my wife)
Week 10: 4
Week 11: 3
Week 12: 4
Week 13: 4
Week 14: 5 (on the last day, I sold three within the space of about three hours)

Summer Total: 69
Earnings: ~$35,000

On this journey through one of the most difficult jobs I've ever had, I got a glimpse into my $300K potential. There were three weeks in a row where I felt on top of the world. I sold almost half of all my accounts during those three weeks. Making about $6,000 a week is what it takes to make $300K a year. I was able to achieve that during weeks when I was hyper-focused on achieving my goals. I knew that if I could have every week like that for the entire year, I could make big-boy money. Since then, I've had $10,000 days, which, if you work six days a week, would result in earning $3,000,000 a year. I haven't figured out the formula to earn that much yet though.

Fortunately and unfortunately, I learned a tough lesson about momentum when I left on vacation right after those incredibly successful weeks. Taking a break and leaving midsummer was directly against the advice my manager gave me, which was to keep working non-stop through the summer. I came back from that trip, and it felt like I was starting over from scratch. I basically had to learn to sell all over again, and oh man, was it rough! I didn't get back into that double-digit flow for the rest of the summer and only experienced a moderate level of success until the time came to head back to school.

The Second Summer in Purgatory

If you think the first summer sounded bad, it was nothing compared to the second summer. We moved ten times in the space of ten weeks. We were living in hotels with a seven-month-old baby who was teething. We were living off of fast food and continental breakfast. Under those circumstances, I learned that when I experience extreme levels of stress, I can have severe anxiety. This stress and anxiety led me to jump out of the car window in the middle of traffic. As a passenger in the car, I wanted us to turn right but my in-laws wanted to turn left. They probably think/know I'm crazy now. On another occasion, I had a panic attack and almost passed out in front of the LDS Baton Rouge Temple. My ID card, or "recommend," that gave me permission to get inside the building had expired a few days earlier, and they consequently couldn't let me in. I pushed the limits of my sanity that summer and somehow survived!

Do you ever have flashbacks to the most miserable times of your life? Do you ever think back to an overly emotional and tough learning moment that almost makes tears well up inside you? I have flashbacks of those wretched summers quite often. I shudder and think, "I'm so glad I'm not doing summer sales anymore!"

Being broken and beaten down is so important in order to be rebuilt better and stronger than before. If you're never subjected to stress, your growth potential is *so* limited. In fitness, if you never lift weights heavy enough to make you a little uncomfortable, you'll never achieve worthwhile weightlifting goals. If you don't get fouled playing basketball, you aren't playing the game right. If you never fall down, trip on a hurdle, fumble, get tackled, pinned, skunked, bruised, body slammed, or spladled and spanked, then you won't fully learn to play the game.

In the end, I finished off the summer with 75 accounts, just barely beating my rookie year. Enduring the challenges I did that summer left me a stronger salesman than ever before and with a future shaped for success.

Why Did I Do a Third Summer???

Why in the world would I subject myself to the agony and torture of another summer down south, sweating my gonads off selling security systems? The months leading up to that last summer were mentally tough. My wife tried to convince me not to go again. She begged multiple times, but to no avail. I was going to prove that I could be one of the best in my company.

My third year, I was right next to the swampy bayous of Lake Charles. You'll never understand my pain if you've never walked from door to door to door to door to door to door to door to door to door . . . in the 100-percent humidity of a

Louisiana July (100-percent humidity, that's a real thing FYI; you almost have to swim in order to walk—or rather, wade—from house to house). I have *never* had such an excruciatingly painful feeling on my thighs. Chafing had never made me feel like I needed a handicapped tag for my car. I was in so much pain that when I went to Walmart with my wife, I was so done with the idea of walking that I felt like I needed to ride the electric wheelchairs. For about a week, I walked like a cowboy who had been riding a horse for too long and had gotten kicked in the groin. I continued to work, wading and waddling from door to door, hoping my bloody thighs wouldn't touch each other.

I ultimately chose to go through this pain and finish a third summer because I didn't see a big enough improvement from year one to year two. I had missed something and I needed to prove my worth. I needed to prove that I had the drive and self-motivation to succeed at one of the most mentally challenging jobs out there. I'd had spurts of big success here and there during the previous years, but I had been inconsistent. My biggest challenge that final year would be to develop a consistency that would help me prove to myself that I could be in sales long term. I needed to prove to myself that I could make great money year round and that I really could skip medical school and maintain the same standard of living that I was hoping for in that career. Two summers wasn't enough for me to consider myself a sales veteran.

That last summer, I averaged eight new alarm accounts a week, averaging $5,000 a week. If I could do that year round, then I would make way more money than any job my college degree ever would have yielded. However, by the end of the summer, you couldn't have given me a commission big enough to motivate me to sell one more alarm system. I left everything on the table; I gave my best effort and then ended my summer-only sales career. I felt like I had graduated from that program and was ready for the next step: year-round work, which would include selling in the bitter cold of winter. If you think selling when it's hot is tough, cold is a whole other beast that discourages even the best salespeople.

That last summer experience felt like a platform that took me from mediocre to exceptional. More so than either of the previous years, that last summer gave me a glimpse of the consistency and long-term perspective required to achieve my biggest, meanest, hairiest, wildest goals. I started my new job, and it felt like I was on vacation; for some reason, it just seemed so much easier mentally because I had to pace myself. I had an extra day off each week, which had felt like a foreign concept before. You mean I only have to work five days?! My personal and family time instantly doubled, and my work-life balance suddenly felt manageable. I had essentially been through a rigorous training program that got me to expect life to be more intense than it typically would be. All those years, it was like I was conditioning for a marathon by running sprints. In so doing, I was learning the discipline and income pace I would need to maintain in order to keep up with the best of the best.

The Spladle, the Piano Teacher, and Alligators

Going door-to-door selling alarm systems may not be for everyone. There are other experiences that will lead to your desired end result. Summer sales wasn't the only experience I had of going through a "path of most resistance." Throughout my life, I've had multiple experiences that have been tough and refining. In high school, I had three main sports that I excelled at; they were wrestling, running, and swimming. Unwittingly, I had various fears and painful experiences when I was growing up that inadvertently helped me succeed at each of those sports:

1. Wrestling

I grew up with a family of wrestlers. When I was a young, very obnoxious pre-teen, I often chose not to obey the orders of my fascist babysitter, Asher, who also happened to be my older brother. When I disrespected the dictator's authority, he would grab me in a headlock, throw me to the ground, and then adeptly put me in a wrestling move called "the Spladle." The Spladle is an advanced wrestling move that is, without question, the most emasculating of all wrestling moves known to mankind. While Asher had me pinned to the ground in this depubertizing wrestling technique, a more obedient minion, my other older brother Barak, would then spank me as hard as he could. This scenario probably happened at least a dozen times a year. Don't you love childhood?

My wife said she went through a similar torturous experience growing up. She recounts tales of when her brother, Brian, would pin her down, proceed to hock a loogie, let his spit slowly hang out of his mouth over her face, and then slurp it back up. She said it didn't slurp up once, and while she was screaming in horror, it dropped right in her mouth. Asher and Brian would've had very successful careers working at Guantanamo or in any counterintelligence. Today, one of them is a correction's officer, and the other is now a neurologist. I guess they're still kind of doing the same thing.

Well, my horribly humiliating spladle experience ended up driving me to practice becoming a better wrestler, so no one could ever do that to me again. The point is, experiencing the hardships prompted me to act. It drove my work ethic, which ultimately drove me to have a successful wrestling career.

2. Running

When I was about six years old, my older sister, Hannah, started teaching me piano. Surprisingly, I didn't learn many piano skills at that time, but instead, I learned to be a good sprinter. I remember multiple occasions when, in the middle or at the start of a piano lesson, I would run away because I dreaded that time having to sit still and practice. In my six-year-old mind, she was a slave driver. I had seen *Ben-Hur*, featuring Charlton Heston, many times, and I felt I could empathize with poor Judah Ben-Hur. It was as if the metronome was a drum beating ever faster while my sister yelled "ramming speed." I learned to run pretty fast thanks to that experience.

3. Swimming

When you fall down while waterskiing or wakeboarding in a Florida lake, there is a good chance an alligator is close by. Those chances are especially high if you fall close to the reeds by the shoreline. I always thought the worst situation was when your skis would fall off, leaving your bare feet to dangle in the water. When this happened to me, I would lift my feet up, thinking some hungry gator might mistake my legs for food. The random bubbles all around me were never very reassuring. I've felt currents in the water before that felt like something much bigger than a fish was swimming beneath me. Alligators are naturally afraid of humans, but every once in a while, someone feeds a gator, which creates a correlation between humans and food. They start to think humans = food. You never know when someone has been feeding them. I was always terrified that my feet would become snacks for the alligators, and every time I got in the boat, I was convinced it was right before one was about to bite me. Imagine that situation but in a lake full of dinosaurs. That basically sums up how I felt, which is why I learned to swim so fast.

Similar to my summer sales experiences, these other stressful situations created the need to improve. How grateful I am for the stresses in life that foster growth.

Starvation and Desperation Yield Creativity and Capitalism

On another note, I've noticed that a lack of resources can actually enhance your mental acuity. Have you ever gone to the fridge or pantry and looked around for something to eat, and it seemed like all you had was condiments, pickles, canned beans, and brown rice? You then close the doors and walk away disappointed. You go about your business for a few minutes and then remember you're starving and need to eat. So, you return to the kitchen to look again, thinking something to eat will magically appear. Who knows, maybe you missed something the first five times you stood there staring hungrily at the almost completely empty shelves . . .

We just had this very experience in our home not too long ago; in fact, it's a sad situation that happens quite often in our family. We know we need to go grocery shopping, but because of grocery store anxiety, we procrastinate as long as possible. (Grocery shopping is one of the most inefficient activities in the world. It makes me feel like a prison convict doing menial or useless work. It's reminiscent of digging ditches just to bury them again. Think about it: you fill a cart full of food while in the grocery store, you then wait in a ridiculously long line, only to unload the contents of your cart onto a conveyor belt. Then you load the food into bags that you put back in that cart, then you go to your car to unload the bags into your trunk. You then drive home only to attempt to take all the bags out of your car at once. You end up dropping a few items along the way as you unload the bags into your kitchen. The final task is now to at least unload the refrigerated or frozen items because you're too exhausted at this point to put everything away. I'll talk about delegation later in this book, and I'll tell you how to avoid these types of situations.) With our most recent foodless experience, we had decided a week earlier that we needed to go shopping but just never made it to the store. Well, we'd somehow eaten every day since then, and with each day, our meals became progressively more creative. I was pretty sure we were going to starve after I spent what felt like half a day going to the pantry and the fridge scavenging for sustenance. Usually when we get to this point, we order food to be delivered or we go out to eat; this brings us out of our malnourished state and gives us enough energy to finally go grocery shopping. Well, on this occasion, we had a violent snowstorm that dropped about sixteen inches of snow in the space of about eight hours. We live on a hill and our drive-way is 450 feet long. We were trapped; no escape in sight. There was no way a delivery person would make it up our driveway. And if we slid down our driveway in our car, there was no way we would get back to the top—we'd already had the experience of carrying our groceries up that wretched driveway in the snow, and we weren't going to repeat that again. We became desperate for a meal that consisted of something other than pickles dipped in mustard. When you're desperate, you suddenly start to see more than you did before: your perception is magnified. The food choices that only hours earlier looked inedible, somehow magically turned into a delicious feast and became a family favorite. Desperation breeds creativity. Almost animalistic instincts kick in, and you suddenly realize that you have tons of options. My wife ended up making a taco salad with brown rice, canned black beans, ground beef with taco seasoning, little bit of lettuce, a few grape tomatoes, salsa, sour cream, last tiny bit of remaining cheese, and canned crushed pineapple. Oh, my goodness, that was fantastic! The pineapple made the meal one of the best meals I'd ever eaten. Had we gone to the store a week earlier, that can of crushed pineapple and those black beans would prob-ably have been confined to the pantry for years and eventually donated when someone ran a food drive.

Likewise, the Great Depression of the 1930s yielded many inventions and in-novations due to hardship:

- Ruth Wakefield ran out of baker's chocolate, and so she cut up a choco-late bar and mixed it with the cookie batter. The chocolate chip cookie was born and she sold the recipe to Nestlé. Can you imagine life without the chocolate chip cookie?!
- J.F. Cantrell opened the first laundromat when he noticed that only the wealthy had access to a washing machine. There are currently over 30,000 laundromats in the U.S., and they bring in billions of dollars in revenue every year.
- The Galvin brothers were desperate for income, and as a result, they designed the car radio, which they sold to car manufacturers. Their car radio company eventually evolved into the tech giant, Motorola.

- People had to get creative with resources and cooked food like meatloaf to make their supplies stretch a little bit further each week. My family eats meatloaf all the time now, just because we like it.

More recently, during the global financial crisis also known as The Great Recession, new companies popped up out of necessity. Individuals adapted to their circumstances and turned their life around with unique inventions and refined business plans. Opportunity came in the midst of despair, and many capitalized on that. Do you need a recession to be creative? Comfort leads to complacency, while dire discomfort leads to discipline, decisions, and dedication to succeed.

Summer sales was the path that made me desperate and consequently created the need for success. In that helpless desperation, humans tend to give more effort than the minimum requirements. We often overshoot the mark, and as a result, we achieve massive results. I'll share more in my chapter on self-discipline about my desperation during one of those summers. Let's just say that desperation made me do everything I possibly could to master my profession so I would never experience that same helpless desperation again.

Pondering on this idea of the Great Depression creativity made me think back to the last 100-plus years, and I realized that these major economic downturns are more common than you might think. The stock market follows a cycle of economic booms and busts. The economic expansions last on average about five years, followed by a roughly year-and-a-half contraction or economic bust. During those pullbacks, people are laid off and forced to think outside the norm. Hence—in the midst of those busts—creativity is born. The major learning and growing happens when times are tough. At the height of crisis, people respond with ingenious solutions, and the economy is restored, fortified and stronger than ever before.

The life of sales is the same. It's a rollercoaster of success and failure. Booms and busts. I can say I learn the most when I've been down and depressed, in the middle of my biggest struggles. My creativity has been the most on point when the conditions necessitate that response. It seems to be a defense mechanism of the human brain. It may be wise to rethink your profession if you have a job that is pretty even-keeled with no big ups and downs. Does your job come with little excitement and little opportunity for disappointment from failing and falling flat on your face? The US economy became a world powerhouse after experiencing the painful era of the Great Depression. Growth comes with growing pains. The more you grow, the more intense the pain *has* to be. You'll cry. Many times. I did. But I can say it's totally worth it! Embrace the lows and know that they are your opportunity to learn, assess, be creative, and return stronger than ever before. Criticize the American capitalistic economic system all you want, but I've never seen another country achieve the wealth and ingenuity that the US has. Likewise, criticize the rollercoaster that is the sales cycle all you want, but I haven't seen many other opportunities that can guide a twenty-six-year-old to make $300,000 in a year!

Chapter 4

One-Liners and Power Moves

Now, going through my personal path of most resistance involved conquering a steep learning curve. Along the way, I learned useful techniques and principles that amplified my proficiency. Whatever industry you're in, there are certain phrases or specific body language that seem to have magic (I'm not referring to strippers, but I guess it could apply). They unlock the desired response, and somehow, they make a sale or the desired result happen. Here are a few of my favorites:

Windows to the Soul

One of the best things that I've ever done is learn how and when to make the right amount of eye contact. All business relationships are based on trust. I believe it's true that the eyes are the window to the soul. There's an almost spiritual connection that takes place when someone asks you a serious question: you pause, look them in the eyes, allowing them to see your integrity and character, and follow up with a verbal response. In order for this to work, your soul and intentions have to be pure. If your only goal is to make money, people have a gift of discernment, a "BS detector," if you will. They can typically spot phonies, insincerity, and greed, causing you to lose others' trust and consequently, any potential sale. Cleanse the inner vessel. Have a higher purpose than financial achievement, and the financial success will follow.

Smile

As I mentioned earlier, in between college semesters, I sold alarm systems door-to-door for three years. My first year, we were in Arkansas. On my very last day working that year, I was so done and ready to go home; I had almost completely checked out. I called my wife to tell her that I hated my life because I had been knocking on doors for five hours without any luck. My wonderful wife responded to my whining and said: "On the next door, smile as big as you can." I reluctantly followed her advice because I didn't think I had anything to smile about, but to my surprise, the next person I talked to invited me right in, and they ended up loving our product and had it installed that night! I followed her advice and smiled as big as I could twice more that night, and I ended up selling three alarms in the space of three hours. That's $500–600 an hour! Not a bad day! Since then, I've used this "trick" many times.

The real secret in this anecdote is that I called my wife. I talked to my favorite person in the whole world, the one who brings me the most joy and happiness. I often call her when I need a boost; she probably thinks the only reason I call her while I'm working is to complain. Little does she know, she's crucial to my success. How would I get along without her?! Her reassuring voice offering unconditional love and support gives me something to smile about.

Along those same lines, I don't work very long hours in a day. If I have to work eight to ten hours, I need a break in the middle of the day. On several occasions, the first half of the day just wears me out emotionally, and I need a reminder about why life is fantastic. I run home for an hour or two, take a rejuvenating nap, eat something that brings me joy (like a corned beef Reuben sandwich!), or my favorite, play with my daughters. When I'm not happy, it's harder to smile, which makes it harder to succeed. So, my solution is to do something that makes me happy. I've read multiple pieces of literature that talk about how the act of smiling alone releases endorphins that actually make you happy, like a runner's high. Sometimes, I need a kickstart to even start smiling. That boost for me is sleep, food, and family. Again, first cleanse the inner vessel, actually become happy, then that outward expression of joy comes naturally.

A smile sets the tone for the conversation. Your tone can completely change the meaning of a conversation. The other person's perception of your intentions is dependent on your facial expressions. That's one reason why emojis have become so popular and even necessary to have a more meaningful conversation via text. If you say, "You're such a loser," versus "You're such a loser :)," there's a 100 percent difference in meaning. Or another example would be the following: my wife asks me how she looks, and I respond, "You look fine." If that's my response, then I'll be sleeping outside in my hammock that night. Whereas, "You look fine ;)" conveys a totally different meaning. A big cheesy smile in verbal rather than written conversations carries even more positive weight. The sound and tone of your voice is totally different when you're smiling and happy. What you say is extremely important; however, the *way* you say it drastically impacts the receptivity and enthusiasm of your customers, spouse, parents, boss, class, congregation, children, patients, employees, team, etc. The best trick I know for improving tone is to smile and mean it. Growing up, my dad used to always tell us we had to eat all the food on our plate, even if we didn't want it or like it. He would say, "Eat all of your food and *smile* while you eat it." I sure do love vegetables now; I wonder if that's what did it.

Tequila Makes Her Clothes Fall Off

When trying to progress a potential sale, you need forward momentum. If that momentum stops, then there's often an awkward silence and sometimes, confusion for both parties involved in the transaction. In order to avoid this discomfort, I've found that certain phrases can and should be plagiarized, copied word for word. These are what I call "one-liners." They should only be taken from the top performers in your industry. It's important that you *don't* imitate people who aren't thriving. There's a specific sentence that I use every single time I talk to someone about my product. Before our customers make any sort of commitment to purchasing our product, we first do an analysis on their home to make sure it will work for us. There's no cost for the evaluation and no commitment until their solar panels are installed. After I've taken a minute or two to explain why I'm at their home, I say verbatim, **"Most people just want to see something in writing to know that they aren't *paying* for anything and that they aren't *obligated* to anything. Do you have a place I can set my iPad down?"** The way this phrase works reminds me of the country song, "Tequila Makes Her Clothes Fall Off." Most times with that almost poetic phrase, it seems to work like tequila to melt away their objections. There are phrases like that for every industry. Find them. The most successful people know them and use them every day. It's such a simple phrase that brings reassurance that they aren't going to be swindled.

> "It *is* signed. It's a signed document. I guess if you have a signed document in your possession, you can't go wrong." —Charlie Brown[8]

Fear of financial loss is often the reason people don't want to listen to you. You have to use that special "tequila" phrase, or a similar phrase applicable to your product, in order to get past that fear. "In economics and decision theory, loss aversion refers to people's tendency to prefer avoiding losses to acquiring equivalent gains: it's better to not lose $5 than to find $5. Some studies have

---

[8]"It's the Great Pumpkin, Charlie Brown," directed by Bill Melendez, written by Charles M. Schulz, aired October 27, 1966, on CBS.

suggested that losses are twice as powerful, psychologically, as gains."[9] (Another reason I've been successful is that I use Wikipedia without shame.) Loss aversion should be addressed before they can bring it up. The biggest objection that I get on a daily basis is, "This sounds too good to be true." Addressing that fear of loss before they have a chance to bring it up makes the potential customer realize that their concerns are common and there is proof that what I'm saying is true. A great number of people have been burned one too many times in the past, and as a result, I have to say something that will reassure them that they won't be losing anything with my product.

The second thing this does is that it provides an extremely effective transition from one point in the sale to the next. I'm usually still outside of someone's home when I say this. After I say this phrase, we typically transition from the doorstep to the decision-making dining room table. This phrase makes it so we don't move to a couch, where we won't be as engaged as we should be. I want the customer looking at the slides on my iPad, I want it to be a natural setting for them to start signing forms. It would be awkward if I had to stand up and hand it to them on the other side of a living room. People tend to avoid making decisions while standing. Think about the difference between ordering fast food at the drive-thru versus having to stand in the line at the restaurant. For some strange reason, I'm personally crazy indecisive when I'm standing, and it takes me forever to decide if it's worth the extra $1.50 for guac, whereas when I go through the drive-thru, I never have a problem choosing the extra-large fries.

The Naked Man

How do you create demand for you or your product? You have to have the attitude that "there's only one of me and there's a lot of you." Tesla Motors accomplished this when they were looking for a site to construct their first Gigafactory.

> At least five states competed to attract Gigafactory by offering tax incentives, cash grants and other methods in the hope of future business; California, Arizona, Nevada, New Mexico, and Texas . . . States without sales tax were topping the list of preferred sites.

(Nevada ended up winning, and as a result, Tesla got some pretty awesome incentives.)

> The incentive package also includes 20 years free from sales tax and 10 years free from property tax . . . By 2034, this package could have accumulated to a value of $1.25 billion in missed taxes.[10]

---

[9]"Loss Aversion," Wikipedia, Wikimedia Foundation, last modified 11 October 2017, 20:27, https://en.wikipedia.org/wiki/Loss_aversion.

[10]"Gigafactory 1," Wikipedia, Wikimedia Foundation, last modified 16 October 2017, 09:53, https://en.wikipedia.org/wiki/Gigafactory_1.

How do you accomplish these results on a daily basis? How do you increase the demand for your business and receive preferential financial treatment? The answer is to pull back. You can't just put it all out there and expect people to want you. People want exclusivity; they want what they can't have. In the TV sitcom, *How I Met Your Mother*, there's a technique I've tried to use called, "The Naked Man." It is "a means of seducing female characters, which is merely surprising them by being naked."[11]

In that episode, Mitch, the character who introduced the "Naked Man" technique, says it works "two out of three times, guaranteed." My personal experience says that's not even close to true; it works maybe 1 out of 100 times. Most of the time, you can't just put it all out there and expect to get your desired results. You have to pull back!

Image 5: The Naked Man

My favorite phrase to use is: **"We'll just tell you 'no.'"** In my industry specifically, there are so many things that could disqualify someone from getting our product; I make sure that all my customers know that. I make sure they understand that my product is an absolute "no-brainer" *if* they're approved, but there's

[11]"The Naked Man (How I Met Your Mother)," Wikipedia, Wikimedia Foundation, last modified 4 May 2017, 05:01, https://en.wikipedia.org/wiki/The_Naked_Man_(How_I_Met_Your_Mother).

a pretty good chance they won't be approved for one reason or another. This builds excitement and intrigue, and they want to know if they make the cut. The way I use the phrase is, "We'll measure/review/inspect your _____; if it isn't good enough, we'll just tell you 'no.'" I simply fill in the blank with "roof," "electrical panel," "sun exposure," "credit score," "transformers," and so on. This can be applied to so many different industries. Every transaction in business has to be mutually beneficial; if it isn't going to benefit you, just say no and walk away!

Don't be tempted to try the Naked Man. Trust my experience, I promise it's better to tell your prospective customer there's a good chance that things might not happen at all. When you approach the proposition this way, it alleviates all the sales pressure. I hate being on any side of a high-pressure sales situation, so I know just about everyone else in the world probably does too.

Bubbles

If you apply the Naked Man principle, you run the risk of having things blow up in your face. If you don't pull back at all and just keep going full throttle, then there's a painful example in financial markets that illustrates what happens. A financial bubble is when the price of an asset is bid up so high, it greatly exceeds the intrinsic value of the underlying asset. Basically, it means people are buying and selling something that is way overpriced. One of the most famous examples is the Holland tulip market in the 1600s. The price of a tulip bulb soared around twenty times in just one year. The price of special or rare bulbs got to be more expensive than the price of a luxurious home. There's an intriguing concept known as the Greater Fool Theory; it asserts that in situations like this Tulipmania, the intrinsic value (which for tulips, should be pennies) doesn't determine price, but rather the market exuberance or irrational belief that someone else will buy your overpriced item for more than you bought it for is what drives the price up. The person who buys it from you is the "greater fool." One greater fool passes off his ridiculously priced item to an even greater fool until eventually, you've found the dumbest person in the land and no one else dumber will buy the asset for a higher price. This is known as a bubble. What happens when you've run out of greater fools? The bubble pops . . . and it pops fast. In the 1600s, the price of tulips plunged 99 percent within the space of a few months back to a fair market price. Ninety-nine PER-flipping-CENT! Betting the family farm on one flower could've completely destroyed someone's lifestyle.

Bubbles aren't healthy. They aren't rational; they embody irrational exuberance for an asset. Sadly, someone always gets burned when irrational exuberance turns to rational capitulation. We've seen massive bubbles pop recently: the Dotcom stock bubble burst in the early 2000s, and the housing market bubble toppled in 2008. Is there a bubble somewhere right now waiting to pop? The following images show the visual difference between a bubble and a healthy bull market that's full of pullbacks:

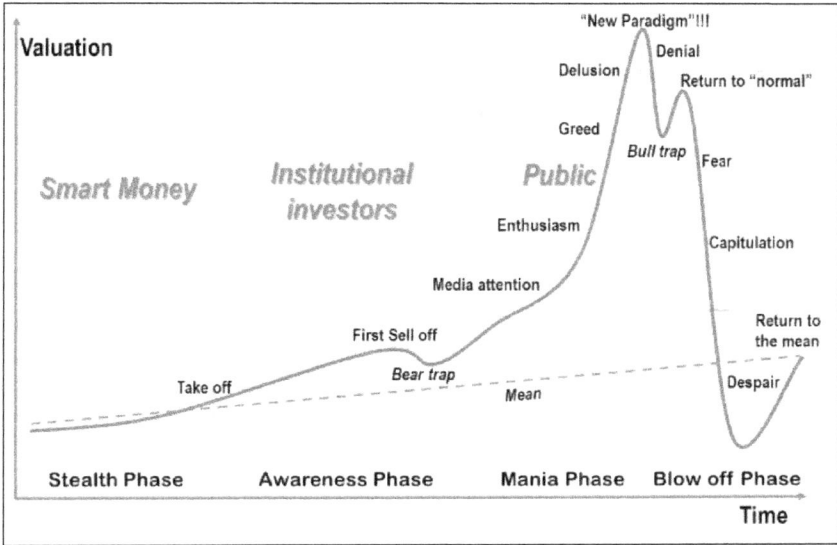

Image 6: Stages in a Bubble[12]

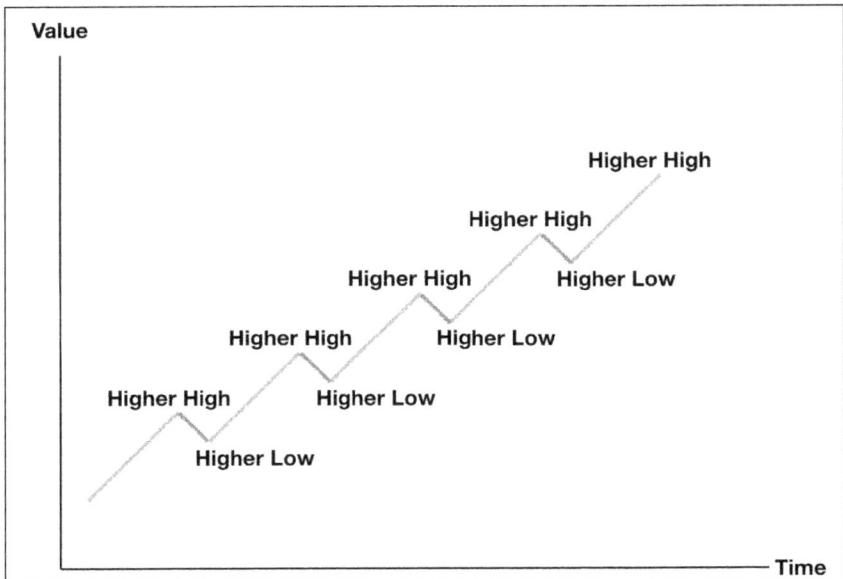

Image 7: Uptrend

[12]"Stages in a Bubble," The Geography of Transport Systems, Dr. Jean-Paul Rodrigue, Dept. of Global Studies & Geography, Hofstra University, https://transportgeography.org/?page_id=9035.

These charts tell a profound story. There's such a stark difference between these two rallies. One is hyperbolic, while the other is linear. One looks like a get-rich-quick scheme, while the other looks like it depicts hard work and delayed gratification. Like hard work, the linear chart looks like it's full of setbacks and disappointments along the way, but always recovering and more determined than before to succeed. Fortunes are destroyed and lives are ruined by the hyperbolic bubbles.

No one wants to be duped into being the greater fool. People have been burned many times before by salesmen, con artists, mechanics, plumbers, general contractors, or even friends and family members. When the thought, "it sounds too good to be true," pops into people's minds, they are haunted by memories of past transactions when they were screwed over. When selling or marketing any product, your job is to build the value of the product to be greater than or equal to the value of the money it costs to buy the product. There's a delicate process to building value with people. If you just give, give, give and there's no pullback, then people smell a bubble, and they walk away because they don't want to be anyone's greater fool. This whole concept is why the phrase, "We'll just tell you no," works so well. Something like that has to be said throughout the sales process. Give a little, but then take some of it back right after. Any exchange of goods or services has to be balanced, it has to make sense. It has to be mutually beneficial and fair. If one party is getting too much in the trade, then something isn't right.

Even if things seem to be going smoothly, a pullback is usually a part of a healthy sales interaction. I want people to be shouting for joy when I call to tell them they're approved for my service because they were expecting to be rejected.

I'm with the Crew

This next one-liner is a personal favorite; it probably accounts for a good third of my new business last year.

I have a bright orange windbreaker that, in my opinion, looks like something a construction worker wears while on the job. I wear it if possible whenever I have a solar installation in a neighborhood. I then go to every single neighbor who can see the big box trucks in front of my customers' homes. My initial sentence is always, **"I'm with the crew working on so-and-so's house."** What does this simple phrase do? First of all, it gives the impression that "I'm just a humble construction worker, and I'm doing work on your neighbor's home, and I just thought I should swing by your home to catch you up to speed on what your neighbor is doing. Your neighbor invited me into the neighborhood so I belong here." Every barrier is down because I'm not perceived as a pesky cockroach of a door-to-door salesman. There is somehow no hesitation or reluctance to listen to me, no smokescreens to get me off their doorstep; after all, who blows off the construction worker working on the house next door?

The combination of that line and the orange jacket accomplishes an attitude that, in my industry, I've come to realize is necessary to adopt. The attitude required to be successful is becoming a metaphorical meter-man. Who tells the meter-man he can't read their meter? No one. What meter-man shies away from going up to a meter and reading it? Not one. There's a crazy level of confidence and a swagger that screams, "I'm supposed to be here." When a salesperson adopts that confidence, it makes them almost unstoppable.

The Eight-Panel Principle

I can easily attribute half of my success to applying several principles in my life. As I was writing this, I realized that it isn't just one secret or phrase, but a combination of many incredible secrets. This is one that I believe is completely necessary. Something I always say to my customers is: **"If we can get at least eight panels on the roof, then it's worth it for us and it's worth it for you."** I'll talk even more about this when I talk about expectations. Basically, you want people to be stoked if they're a qualified buyer for your product. This goes perfectly with the phrase, "We'll just tell you 'no.'" If we can't do the minimum, then sorry, we can't do business. This is more than a pullback, though; this is also setting up a proper expectation for when I return with a proposal. If I don't meet that expectation, for whatever reason, then suddenly in my customer's eyes, I've failed to do my job, and unfortunately, their enthusiasm dissipates. If we get more than that minimum, then they're high-fiving each other and stoked for what lies ahead.

Painting a Picture

I believe that one of the greatest teachers of all time was Jesus Christ. Putting theological differences aside, he has positively impacted more people than anyone else in history; his sphere of influence is larger than any other human to ever walk on the planet. One way that he achieved this is that he taught to the understanding of his humble audience. He employed a teaching tool known as the parable. A parable is a simple story that illustrates a valuable lesson or proves a moral point. As a result of this teaching method, the gospel he taught has spread far and wide to all ends of the earth, and to this day, thousands of years later, billions of people reference and learn from Christ's parables. He painted a simple picture that helped his followers understand and remember what he taught. There are many other great teachers who have employed similar teaching tools. Aesop's fables are one such example. Who hasn't heard of the story of the Tortoise and the Hare? Morals are so much easier to remember when a story or comparison to something familiar is attached to the lesson.

Likewise, I've learned to have multiple analogies to use on a daily basis. They help paint a clear picture that helps my customers remember what I taught them in the middle of the sales cycle. Painting a picture can effectively be used to clear up confusion about points that are often the most difficult objections for prospective customers to overcome.

As previously mentioned, the biggest hang-up or sticking point many of my customers have is that they think my product sounds too good to be true. We're able to switch their electricity supply from the traditional source to rooftop solar energy, and as a result, their electric bill will drop 30–40 percent. It doesn't cost them anything up front to switch over. We pay for tens of thousands of dollars of equipment, the installation, monitoring, maintenance, and insurance for twenty years. I'm constantly asked: "Why would your company pay for all that? Why hasn't everyone already done this if it's that good? What's in it for your company?" Those thoughts cross through almost all my customers' minds. I try to answer them before they can ask those questions out loud. I say something along the lines of:

> I get this question from everyone—they want to know how we make our money. The answer is pretty simple: we make our money the exact same way the utility company makes their money, by producing electricity and delivering it to your property. The only difference is our cost to deliver the power is a lot lower because the power only has to travel a matter of feet versus the traditional way, which has to travel sometimes hundreds of miles. I have a customer who lives down the street who is a firefighter. He thought of this example: imagine you have two firehoses. One is ten feet long and the other is 1,000 feet long. You turn both of them on. Which one will have the stronger flow at the end? It's absolutely the shorter one! The other would probably just have a trickle come out the other end. It's the exact same thing with our electricity; having solar is like having a ten-foot hose. That's why it's cheaper.

What a simple explanation! I know it works because after I say that, you can tell they understand the concept. As the analogy sinks in, their posture changes from defensive and tense to relaxed and ready to hear more and move forward. In this moment, the idea clicks in their mind and it just makes sense. One of the best parts about analogies like that is when that same concern comes up again, I can say: "Remember when I talked about the fire hose? Yeah, that's why it's cheaper." Because that simple picture was painted the first time, they remember the concept every time! Another thought is, what if they talk with a family member who has the same doubt, and they also think my product sounds too good to be true? Well, my customer is equipped with a simple, easy-to-remember analogy that answers that concern when anyone brings it up.

People buy based on emotions and then justify that purchase using logic. It's so important to have a simple, logical picture painted that helps people prove to themselves that they made a good decision. It doesn't matter what profession you're in, people will always have concerns about your product. Take the biggest ones, and simplify them down so a child can understand the answer to the objection. That simplification in the form of a mental image melts the objection away, allowing a transaction to occur.

I want my customers to be pretty much decided on my first visit with them that if they get approved for my product, then they're moving forward. I just recently used another analogy to help my customer realize what a no-brainer my product is if their home gets approved for it. I said something along these lines:

> We're decentralizing electricity production, helping more people get their power locally. I'm a huge believer that food is *way* better the more local it is. My favorite food in the world comes from a homegrown garden. There are no GMOs, preservatives, or pesticides. It's just pure organic deliciousness. There's nothing like plucking a tomato right off the vine, slicing it up and sprinkling it with sea salt and fresh ground black pepper. The only problem is, I hate taking care of a garden with all the deer, rabbits, ants, weeds, and blood, sweat, and tears required to take care of it. No, thank you! What we're doing with our product is that we're saying you don't have to get your food from the store anymore. We'll plant a garden in your backyard and take care of everything for you. We'll weed it, water it, do everything. You just buy the food from us at a 40-percent discount versus the grocery store.

Who would say no to having someone plant and maintain a garden in their yard? I would take that in a heartbeat! Painting a picture is worth more than a thousand words.

The Polite Way to Say, "Let Me Speak First"

In every cold-calling sales encounter, there's a certain point when I feel like I almost have to steamroll my customers with vital information. I feel like they need to have a firm understanding of what I am proposing. If they don't give me the time of day, then I'll never have the chance to educate them, which means I'll never have the chance to build the perceived value of my product. Learning to control a situation is a vital life skill that I began learning years ago. When I was on the racquetball team in college, I spent hours learning the strategy of the sport. The most important technique I learned was to control the center of the court. That one strategy makes it easier to play offensively, rather than defensively. The offensive player decides where the ball goes; the defensive player only has time to react and in many cases; just barely returns the pass. When watching an exchange between two players, it's almost comical to see one player playing offensively, forcing the other player to play defensively. One player is running around like a madman diving for the ball, running into walls, and almost doing the splits. Their shots are usually very high, slow, poorly placed, and easy to return. On the other hand, the offensive player puts the ball right where they want it and has plenty of time to react to the poorly placed defensive shot by their opponent.

Sales interactions are no different; the person who metaphorically takes control of the center of the court has the upper hand. You have to assume control, establishing your role as a teacher and guide. I say the following phrase every single time I'm in an appointment with a client: **"I have a few things to go over, which should answer 90 percent of your questions."**

This basically says, "I have the answers to all your questions; if you listen for a few minutes, I'll answer all of them, so you don't even have to ask them." This statement implies that I get a lot of the same questions and that I understand they are confused or clueless at this point. It's key to note that the tone of my voice when I say this is extremely respectful and almost asking for permission to proceed forward. I've rarely had people refuse to let me speak after I use that phrase. On rare occasions, they try to stop me mid-presentation because they think they already know everything about my product. In those cases, I ask a handful of questions just to double check their understanding, and then I proceed, still addressing the most important points that I'm positive they've never heard. I just condense my presentation as much as possible.

How to Get Enough Referrals to Last a Lifetime

This next one-liner is absolutely beautiful. I can't express how incredible it makes the sales process. I started using this, and my enthusiasm and love for my job doubled instantly. The neatest part about it is that my customers' attitudes and enthusiasm toward my product also doubled. Before I share the phrase, I'd like to give a note of caution. This phrase will not be nearly as effective if you don't refine your presentation to be simple and easy for your customers to understand. By using this line, you'll essentially create a bunch of clones of yourself. If you're confusing, your customers will most likely be confusing too. This phrase comes from an extremely talented individual who is probably the best referral generator I've ever known, Adam McClellan. He gave my whole region a training on a conference call early one Saturday morning where he shared this phrase, and right away, I knew it would be a total game changer. Basically, the wisdom he shared was this: when you're wrapping up your initial contact with your customer, setting up a time to get a bid put together, you say, **"If you refer five other people who also get proposals done with us before your system gets installed, we'll pay for your first year of service."** This instantly became a staple in my interaction with every customer. The first time I tried it, the conversation went something like this:

> **Me:** Our company just came out with this new incentive where we pay for your first year of solar if you refer five people before you get your panels installed. They don't have to necessarily get it, they just have to get their home surveyed.
> **Customer:** Oh, I can think of two people right now!

My customer was ready to start selling for me right then and there! They weren't even sure if they were getting my product yet, but they were ready to get other people on board. So, even if that customer wasn't approved or ultimately decided not to do it, at least they would have given me a referral who could potentially move forward and buy.

Another major benefit of using this line is that it solidifies the customer. Once someone shares a product or service with someone else, their commitment to that product or service goes up exponentially. It would be pretty strange to refer someone to a company that you yourself aren't going to use. So, even though this one-liner is used on the first step of the sale, that customer is going to be way more likely to move forward once they have a proposal. A year of free service is no small deal. Now keep in mind, these are numbers that happen to work great for my industry; that year figure will need to be adjusted based on the product and industry. If a sales presentation doesn't include something like that on the first visit, it needs to be added. It should be something that sets the sale up for the close *and* repeat business. The first interaction with the customer is so important; you have to have a DTR, you have to define the relationship. They have to know from the moment you meet them that you will have a long and healthy, mutually beneficial relationship. Once that's established, the referral business will flow in with little to no effort.

5 Choose Your Circle of Five Deliberately—It Takes a Village to Raise a Millionaire

Follow the Positive, Avoid the Negative

> "A merry heart doeth good like a medicine: but a broken spirit drieth the bones."[13]

As successful as I've been, I'm surrounded by people who have achieved significantly better results. I would be remiss not to acknowledge the people who have helped me get to my current state. There's a saying that I first heard from the renowned motivational speaker, Jim Rohn, that has been eternally ingrained in my mind. He said, "You are the composite, or average, of the five people who you spend the most time with." My college sales professor had us do an exercise where we evaluated our circle of five individuals who had the biggest influence on our life. We were supposed to identify our best, most valuable influences. We were assigned to write out how we could spend more time with them and learn to better emulate them. Then we were then told to identify any "toxic" relationships—people who it would've been better to purge from our lives. This was such an eye-opening process that completely changed the direction of my life.

---

[13]Prov. 17:22

Do you have people you interact with who need to be eliminated from your life entirely? Drop them! Move across the country! Break free from the shackles of your naysayers and critics; your burdens will be lifted, and you'll have room to breathe and achieve. Is there someone telling you your dreams and goals are impossible? Even if it's nonverbally, they are toxic and have no place in your Circle of Five.

We recently followed one of my coworkers across the country. I had so much confidence in his ability to train me and help me succeed that I uprooted my family. We left our comfort zone and moved over 2,000 miles away from our nearest family. We left perfect winter weather of Arizona for the polar vortex of Connecticut. We were welcomed to the area by some of the top talent in the solar industry. I now live in an area where I have 100-percent confidence in the leadership, a group comprised of some of the most talented and all-around solid leaders I've ever met. I know that if solar energy completely disappeared suddenly, this group wouldn't skip a beat. They would work together on something new and totally dominate that new industry. I've been able to immerse myself in a group of individuals who have a culture of winning. Simply because of my association with this culture, I now expect myself to succeed. I can't quit until I conquer the challenges facing me; otherwise, I won't fit in.

Every once in a while, we have a sales rep pass through our office who has a negative energy. You can almost feel a black hole surrounding their aura: they rarely smile, their comments are negative, and you feel negative after talking to them. They are energy suckers! They barely give at all and only seem to take. They want big results with little or no effort. These energy suckers should be avoided at all costs. Don't hire them, don't work with them; only work with the most positive and upbeat people you can find. There are plenty of fish in the sea; do you want to hang out with the bottom feeders or the whales, sharks, and dolphins? You can choose to spend your time with the chronic whiners, the Negative Nancies, and the Debbie Downers, *or* you can surround yourself with the go-getters, the movers and shakers, the elite, the ones who rule the ocean of life.

Multiple Circles of Five

It's vital to choose the right people to look to for guidance. Some people have expertise in certain areas of life and are specialists in that particular topic. It's important to ask for help from those experts when trying to make a positive decision.

Certain individuals are great support in some areas but horrible in others. My life is pretty fantastic but it's far from perfect. We have tons of first-world problems. Here's an example of someone not fitting into a circle of influence: my mother-in-law just visited us for a week and for whatever reason, took an entire party-sized bowl of salad comprised of lettuce, tomatoes, and cucumbers, and because "the trash can was full," she dumped it down the sink and tried to put it down the garbage disposal. Needless to say, it clogged pretty badly. My sweet mother-in-law then tried to blame our pipes. Bahahaha! Don't accuse my pipes when you dump a whole freaking bowl of salad down my sink! As I'm sure you can imagine, my mother-in-law is *not* in my Circle of Five for making plumbing decisions. However, my mother-in-law is one of the most compassionate human beings on the planet. She grew up in the streets of Annapolis, Maryland, living in poverty, raised by a single mother; she knows how it feels to be in need. This experience has helped her to thrive in her career as a family counselor for the Air Force. She's able to offer profound insight, empathy, and wisdom to her clients. A rule of thumb for therapists is to not therapize your family—well, she broke the rule once at a time when I really needed it, and that love and guidance helped strengthen my relationship with her beautiful daughter.

I have groups of people whom I follow for career advice, but I'd never want to follow their religious or marital advice, or vice versa. Just because someone has great work success but a crappy marriage, or the opposite, that doesn't mean I can't have them in my life. I've learned to screen the advice I receive. It's so important to take the good and filter out the bad. Although, I do think it is important to avoid including people in any circle of influence who are seriously struggling to balance their life, because part of that instability may inadvertently rub off on you.

We have several areas of life that go into creating the overall human life experience. It's important to have mentors or guides in each area who are the best of the best. If you only have friends who are good at one or two areas, like finances and health, you'll probably be just the same. In a stock portfolio, if you only have high-flying equities and the market tanks, your entire portfolio will tank. Just like a stock portfolio, you need to diversify your friends and influences. Have a group of sincerely spiritual and religious friends that you council with for spiritual matters. Have a group of financial experts to assist with financial decisions. It's important to realize that you and your spouse may not be in every single one of each other's Circle of Five for every category, and that's okay. I think it would be awesome to have that, though; maybe one day, I'll work out enough to be in her fit circle.

Whom Do I Talk To?

Like I said, it's so important to have a council of people to whom you look for advice in different aspects of life. I have different people who influence me in categories such as financial, spiritual, emotional, physical, and social. A great example of this is that when talking finances, there are certain people I work with whom I really enjoy talking to. One of them is my accountant, Barbara. Barbara is like-minded when it comes to money. It's really neat to talk with her because I feel like I can have a completely open financial conversation with her because she knows, just as well as I do, how much money I have coming in and leaving my accounts. I lucked out hardcore, though, with hiring her, because she not only does my taxes, she's also extremely interested in educating people and helping them actually understand what's going on with their taxes and finances. Another person that I can be open with is my financial advisor. It's really nice to have someone to talk to who is used to working with people who make my caliber of income. Find those types of people in your life, people who help you make smart decisions.

Other people I really enjoy talking with are similar income earners. People attract similar people, so it's easy to come off as a douchebag (pardon my French) if you talk to people about how much money you make and they're nowhere near the same level. I wouldn't be comfortable at a billionaire cocktail party, and I wouldn't be comfortable at a homeless shelter for the same reason. In either setting, I would stick out like a sore thumb. For this reason, I think upward mobility is a tough feat for many. I've heard a number of inspirational rags-to-riches stories where individuals left their humble surroundings and made it big. Eric Thomas, "the hip-hop preacher" is a prime example of that life transformation. Those drastic life improvements are rare, though, because it's easier to stick with what and whom you know. If you're surrounded by chronic underachievers and that's all you've ever known, then the path of least resistance is to perpetuate the complacency of your peers. How can you move up? For that reason, I talk with similar income earners, but usually someone who is a step or two ahead of me. I seek them out intentionally and am genuinely interested in them because I want to be like them.

I am always asking for book recommendations from people who are more successful than I am; I'll go more into depth about the incredible impact of reading good literature in a later chapter. I've read so many books that have shaped my success. If someone is more successful than I am, it's probably because they're doing something I'm not. If I imitate the most successful people, learning the same principles and developing the same skills, then I believe there's no reason I can't match their success. We're all human beings; we all breathe the same air and have access to many of the same resources. I recently had a perfectly candid, two-hour conversation with one of my mentors. I am extremely grateful for the wisdom that he shared with me. He reminded me of the truly affluent mindset of humility that has helped me get to where I am today. During that conversation, he talked me out of buying a car I knew I shouldn't purchase. He recommended what is now one of my all-time favorite books, *The Millionaire Next Door*. To top it off, his sage advice molded and positively reshaped my paradigm about money. If I didn't seek out and glean knowledge from people wiser and more experienced than myself before making huge life decisions, I wouldn't be where I am today. My success is not a product of my own talent and knowledge, but rather it's a product of what I've learned and adopted from others. I've never even met the majority of the people who have completely transformed my life. I gain a significant portion of my knowledge from reading and studying the best literature available. In so doing, I've been able to invite complete strangers into my circle of influence through the media they produce. That's one reason why I wrote this book; I've been so blessed by others, I'd like to pay it forward. If you'll have me, through the teachings in this book, I'd like to be in your circle of influence and help you become your truly best self.

Bigger and Better

I absolutely love life! There's so much joy to be had in each and every day. There's no reason to be surrounded by unnecessary negativity. As I was reflecting on my experience in developing a $300K @ 26 lifestyle and mentality, I was reminded of a unique game called "Bigger and Better." You may not be familiar with the game, so I'll explain it briefly. A time limit is set for a handful of hours. You divide your group into teams. Each team gets a small object, like a pencil or a paperclip, with the instructions to go door-to-door, attempting to trade the initial item for a "bigger and better" object. With each door, the object gradually gets slightly better than the previous object. People have traded up to eventually having bicycles and stereo systems, and there are even legends of people trading up so well that they finished with a working car.

Can and should this game be applied to relationships? (The first time my wife read this, she was not happy; she said that I better not think that it applies to marriage! Maybe in certain cases, spouses can apply, but that's the exception, not the rule.) Is it possible to live life gradually picking and choosing new friends and coworkers who are, with each subsequent acquaintance, just a little better, a little smarter, a little richer, a little more balanced, a little healthier, a little happier? Why not? Life is governed by the laws of nature, and nature has many examples of slow changes that compound into major improvements or adaptations. The evolutionary process is an example of very gradual improvement that animals undergo. Natural selection runs its course and the fittest survive. The changes and mutations in evolution take generations to fully change a species. Well, no one wants to wait for generations to be wealthy. I personally want to be well off and successful in my lifetime. *Deliberate selection* rather than natural selection of friends, coworkers, family, workout buddies, etc. has helped put me on the fast track to success by surrounding myself with others who embody success.

Who do you want to be like? Follow them, emulate them, learn everything you can from them. If they don't keep improving, then add someone new to your circle of influence who is better than you, and chase them. I'm not necessarily saying to drop people altogether once you surpass them—it is important to maintain loyalty and friendship. However, you need to make sure your group's average is always in an uptrend of improvement. Once you get to a certain point where your Circle of Five is extremely like-minded and goal-oriented, they will probably improve right alongside you.

Look at your peers. Think about their impact on your pocketbook. Are you surrounded by high achievers? If you want to make great money, you have to trade out the lethargic and underachieving for people who are "bigger and better." You definitely have to drop the naysayers for people who are "bigger and better." In my opinion, you can and should drop people from your circle of influence even if they're family. I'm not in any way advocating divorce; your spouse may want nothing to do with finances or making money, and I think that's okay. It's okay if your spouse isn't in every single circle of influence of your life. I'm not in my wife's circle of influence for fitness, and that's why she's in such fantastic shape! Eventually, I would love to be, but I'm not at her level yet, and I don't really deserve to be in that circle of influence; I would probably bring her average *way* down. You don't work out with vegetating couch potatoes if you want to be a supermodel. Likewise, you don't spend time with moochers, gamblers, and idlers if you want to be financially free.

Take some time right now to analyze your Circle of Five and make the changes you need to be successful.

6 Maybe Skip School

Learn from the Best

Who teaches? In *School of Rock*, Jack Black said, "Those that can't do, teach, and those that can't teach, teach gym."[14] Agreed. I have, however, seen a handful of exceptions to this. I had three professors in my final semester of college who did *not* come from academic backgrounds. None of them had a PhD, but rather they were all incredibly successful at their careers in the "real world." One of my professors was a retired hedge fund manager who needed something to do, so he taught a stock trading class. Another of those professors worked at UL as a head of global sales, and he was moonlighting as a sales teacher because he loved teaching and sharing his philosophies of success. The other professor had been a lawyer in Venezuela, and she taught advanced Spanish translation after she had experienced years of successful application in that field. Those three classes were structured so differently from the normal pattern of my entire college experience. The focus wasn't the next test; we rarely even had tests. I never even studied for a test. I wasn't learning to prepare myself for an exam, I was

---

[14]*School of Rock*, directed by Richard Linklater, 2003.

learning to learn. What an interesting concept! For some reason, that makes so much sense, but it's almost totally unheard of in our current public educational model. It almost seemed like a huge chore for those professors to even have an exam; they preferred to just teach us to apply the material we discussed. The main objective those three cared about was real-world application, and nothing else mattered; their experience in the field had reinforced that notion. Every assignment we did was practical; I never felt like we were assigned to complete mindless "busy" work.

There are traditional teachers who really stand out and make a difference, though they've been few and far between in my experience. What difference would it make if you chose to learn from someone who is at the top of their industry, instead of focusing all your learning in the traditional classroom?

I recently had a sit-down with the billionaire founder of my company. My biggest takeaway from that conversation was that he doesn't read books written by anyone who isn't already successful. That idea really struck a chord with me. It made me realize that theories and philosophies are nice, but when you haven't actually done what you're teaching, your credibility is shot.

This book is about how to be off-the-charts successful, rather than average. It's about developing that $300K @ 26 mentality. With that in mind, I'm absolutely positive that reading has taught me way more than formal schooling. I'm willing to bet there is a direct correlation between the number of books you read every year and your income. I've noticed in my own life that when I'm reading uplifting literature, I'm successful and accomplish more. When I take a break from reading, my success and momentum seem to grind to a halt. What you're reading, however, is far more important than how much you're reading. In 2014, there was an article published in *Business Insider*, titled, "What Rich People Have Next to Their Beds." The findings were profound.

Here's how the numbers break down:

- 11 percent of rich people read for entertainment, compared to 79 percent of poor
- 85 percent of rich people read two or more education, career-related, or self-improvement books per month, compared to 15 percent of poor
- 94 percent of rich people read news publications including newspapers and blogs, compared to 11 percent of poor people[15]

Zig Ziglar once said, "Rich people have small TVs and big libraries, and poor people have small libraries and big TVs."[16] Is this an example of a correlation or

[15]Libby Kane, "What Rich People Have Next to Their Beds," accessed October 16, 2017, http://www.businessinsider.com/rich-people-read-self-improvement-books-2014-6.
[16]Western, "34 Best Zig Ziglar Quotes on Leadership."

causation? Without a doubt, causation! You don't need to run a study to prove this point; I absolutely know that there has been an incredible impact on my life from the wisdom of the hundreds of books I've absorbed and applied in my life.

Activation Energy

The wealthy seem to read incessantly, so this begs the question, what do good books actually do? How do they work to ameliorate the success of the most successful? This might get a little nerdy for a minute—remember, I was a cum laude chemist in a past life. I'm going to relate what I've personally experienced from reading uplifting and educational literature to a principle I studied in my chemistry and biology courses.

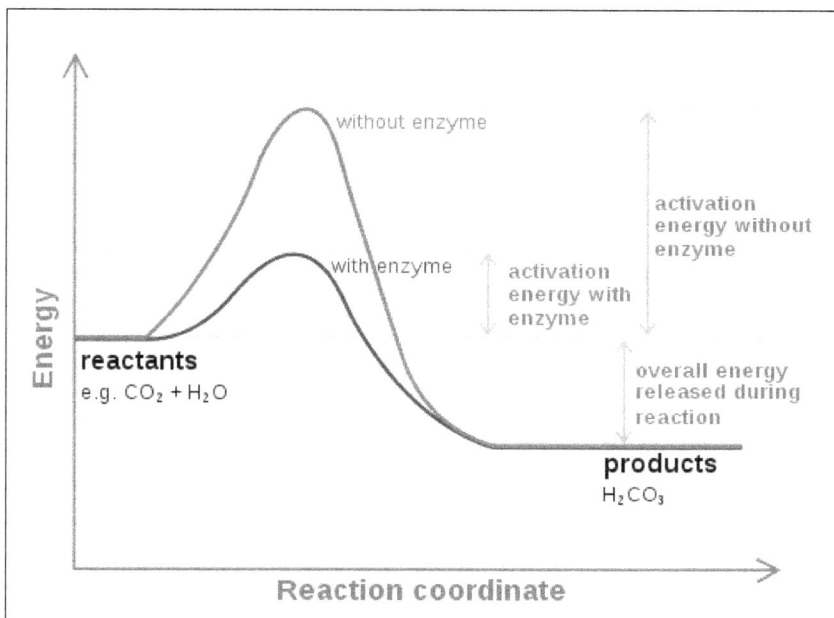

Image 8: Activation Energy[17]

"Activation energy" is the energy required to move a chemical reaction forward to completion. This energy could include actions like adding heat or increasing pressure. Some reactions are spontaneous and happen effortlessly, like mixing vinegar with baking soda, while other reactions require extremely high levels of energy in order to make something happen. Some reactions even require a catalyst. In most cases, though, once you get over that initial hump, the reaction generally coasts through the rest of the process. Think of the shape of the above graph as being a lit-

---

[17]"Activation2 updated.svg" by Jerry Crimson Mann is licensed under the Creative Commons Attribution-Share Alike 3.0 Unported license.

eral rollercoaster. You have to spend a ton of energy pushing and pulling your way to the top of that peak, and once there, you can speed down to the bottom effortlessly.

Making exorbitant amounts of money is *not* spontaneous; it's *not* like mixing vinegar and baking soda. It has an extremely high activation energy, meaning that the climb to the top of the peak is steep. You often need to add a catalyst, which in chemical reactions is what lowers the amount of energy needed to get over that hump. It's what makes that top line transform into the bottom line.

We all need a catalyst to get the results we want. Everyone has a different catalyst; a universal catalyst is reading. The amount of mental energy required to succeed is lowered substantially. This is because certain books produce a newfound positivity, and the reader often gains a better understanding of how the world works. Additionally, there are so many people who have trail-blazed through different professions, failing repeatedly before they eventually learn how to be successful in their field. Why waste the time failing on your own when you can learn from others' mistakes? Read books written by business magnates, high achievers, and people who dedicate their time to researching and interviewing the rich and successful. Those who have forged ahead and found the path to success know the catalysts necessary to lower the effort required for big results in their industry. Every generation should be able to thrive economically faster and faster than previous generations. One generation learns from the mistakes of their predecessors and then adds their input on improvements. Then they pass on the new and improved wealth of knowledge to their successors. If done in this manner, every generation should be better than the previous one. Winston Churchill famously said, "The farther back you can look, the farther forward you are likely to see." If you look back, you can predict the future pretty accurately. Given the data from people previously in your situation, you can extrapolate almost exactly what needs to be done to reach your desired outcome. It's likely that someone already had many of the problems that are preventing you from reaching your goals. It's also likely that someone figured out how to solve those problems. School teaches you that looking at someone else's paper and copying them is cheating. Life outside school necessitates you copying your neighbor, and in fact, it's encouraged. Reading a book about someone else's success and failures is quite similar to taking a class with the benefit of having a previous student's notes. Reading the right books is like having the chance to study the teacher's answer key. It's so much easier to succeed when you have the correct answers going into the test. Life is one big test, and some people have already figured out a lot of the right answers. Much of my success is attributable to the books I've read.

What I Read

Do you remember taking a class that made you feel like you were actually learning something? What was different about that class? For me, there was a distinct difference between those classes and the ones where, to this day, I fail to remember much about them. The ones that I didn't choose to take, the "required" courses were usually always the ones where I would just memorize the information to pass the exams. I was pretty sure I would never use it again, so I packed the majority of the coursework into my short-term memory, and after test day, it disappeared. I didn't want to truly learn that information because I didn't want to clog my long-term memory with unimportant and inapplicable teachings. In my experience, they were also classes in which I had no interest.

I consider myself a scholar because I love to learn. Yet, in my formal educational experience, I realized that learning and schooling are not always synonymous. Learning is an extremely enjoyable experience; school is often the opposite. I have read way more books outside of school than what I read while in school, because *I chose* the subject and author. On top of that, I also chose the medium; I typically listen to books rather than read them in print because that's how I enjoy them the most.

I want to share with you a list of some of the books that have influenced me the most in my life and career. There were many required books in school; however, not one of them influenced me more than any of the books on the following list. These have all been extraordinary catalysts in my life and have, in many cases, changed the entire course of my life.

1. *The 21 Irrefutable Laws of Leadership*. I set a goal when I first started working at my company to be promoted to a management position within my first year of employment. I didn't kick my work ethic into gear until after I read this book. I realized that I needed to basically be performing the duties of the job I was pursuing without any additional compensation. When I realized and internalized that principle, I was promoted months sooner than I had anticipated; when the time came to fill the position, I was the natural choice to be promoted. I had basically claimed the position by doing most of the tasks without being paid. Another gem I uncovered in this book was the Law of the Big MO. I attribute much of the huge success I've had to creating big momentum. I stopped jumping around from area to area, looking for better opportunities and greener grass, and instead chose to water and fertilize the soil where I was planted. What a difference that consistency and momentum made! To illustrate this point, the author, John Maxwell, talks about how a freight train at a standstill can be prevented from moving forward by a pair of relatively small wooden blocks. On the flipside, if you take that same train and give it some good momentum, charging down the tracks at 80 mph, then it will bust right through a steel wall. When I've been discouraged by an overwhelming urge to pick up and move somewhere else, only to start all over, I hear the sage, all-knowing tone of John Maxwell's voice. I imagine him encouraging me to keep the course and patiently build momentum, promising that if I do so, I'll reap the greatest results. I consequently stay put and work harder than ever. I recently bought a house specifically to commit myself to Big MO; it forced me to stay in the same sales territory for years. Without committing to MO, the conditions wouldn't have been right for reaching that $300K income.

2. *How to Win Friends and Influence People.* I read the first half of this book on my flight en route to propose to my wife. Oh, what a difference just reading *half* of it made! My future in-laws were all in love with me because I was practicing all the principles I learned from this book. This book is the Bible of personal development. If you haven't read it yet, add it to your wishlist right now. This is an absolute must-read; it's the textbook that teaches you how to live a good life. Many of the principles in *$300K @ 26*, like smiling in Chapter 4, were influenced by *How to Win Friends and Influence People.* Simple changes in your behavior and word choice make a world of difference. This book has hundreds of anecdotes from the lives of some of the greatest leaders our country has ever known. Following those anecdotes, the book shares real-world results from your average everyday person trying to emulate the greats. The principles are tested and they work like magic. The main thesis of this book is how to make life richer and more meaningful by striving to become a genuine, thoughtful human being. This crowning achievement of the author, Dale Carnegie, has already made it into the hands of tens of millions of individuals; the world would be a much better place if it were read by tens of millions more.

3. *The Happiness Advantage.* As I was reading this book, I started playing a game with strangers wherever I went: I would see how many people I could get to crack a smile. Multiple strangers at the grocery store? Check. Sales clerk at a gas station? Check. Three-year-old daughter? She was the hardest person to get to smile, but now she loves playing the "smile game," as she calls it. The most memorable idea I took from the book was: Genuinely smile at people for at least seven seconds. When you do, it's virtually impossible for them not to smile back![18] Challenge accepted! This fun book was an important element in shaping the person I'm deciding to become. Money is useless without first creating joy in your life. Happiness is scientifically a choice, it all depends on which "bits" of information we choose to look for. This book helped me to not only *expect* the best-case scenario to play out but also actively *search* for it.

4. *Extreme Ownership.* I've had the problem of trying to cast blame off myself for years. When you realize that you're in control of way more than you think, and accept that responsibility, big things start to happen. There's always someone who's working harder than you, someone to chase. The co-author, Jocko Willink, is one of those people for me. Talk about determination and discipline. As a former Navy SEAL, he is on such a high level of discipline and leadership, I can't help but want to follow him. Google him, he's insane—in a good way. The book references a SEAL training exercise where the class is split into smaller groups and then assigned to race each other in lifeboats. One group in the class repeatedly performed horribly, so the teacher changed the leader in the boat crew. That one change determined the success of that team. This book made me realize that as a leader, you are *required* to accept 100-percent responsibility for the

---

[18]Shawn Achor, *The Happiness Advantage: The Seven Principles of Positive Psychology That Fuel Success and Performance at Work* (New York: Crown Business, 2010), 186.

success or failure of your team. Once a leader assumes extreme ownership, the team will follow suit and assume extreme ownership. Teams will perform exceptionally better when they own the results rather than seek to blame someone else for their shortcomings. As the book said, there are "No bad teams, only bad leaders."

5. *Be Obsessed or Be Average.* This one inspired me to write the book you're reading right now. I realized that if the half-insane, eccentric Grant Cardone with his swaggered Louisiana drawl can write an incredible book, then heck, so can I! I was only halfway through reading his book when I started writing this one. His message fueled my obsession; it fueled my excitement and enthusiasm to create a work that would change people's lives. During the first thirty days of writing my book, I didn't get great sleep. Make that ninety days. I wrote quite a bit during the day, maybe a couple hours here and there. I wanted to come home for lunch breaks not to feed my body, but to feed my obsession to write. It was all I could think about as I worked, and then every night, I wrote religiously from 11 pm to 2 am. Before I started writing *$300K @ 26*, I would normally go to bed around 11 pm, but that all changed when the hunger to write began. When I was ready to go to sleep, I would take a supplement called valerian extract that was supposed to help me fall asleep, and then I would start writing in my book. About thirty to sixty minutes in, almost out of nowhere, an uncontrollable desire to do something great was left unsatisfied—unless I wrote till my mind nearly shut off from exhaustion.

Very early on in the writing process, I felt self-conscious about writing at all. I felt silly about the whole thing, thinking, "Who would even read this?" These thoughts lingered in my mind and I almost stopped completely. Then, again, out of nowhere, there was a section in Grant's book where it felt like he was talking directly to me; he told me to ignore the "naysayers" when writing a book. He said, "Haters are going to hate, while the obsessed are going to create."[19] People who don't do, don't write books. Another gem came at the moment when I doubted myself the most and was ready to quit: "I can't tell you how many times I've told someone I'm writing a book and their response is, 'You know, it's a lot of work to write a book,' or, 'People don't read books anymore,' or, 'Did you know that most books never get published?' This is the voice of the naysayer who needs to make sense of not doing, who needs to defend their right to be average. They've never written that book they've always wanted to write!"[20] This couldn't have come at a better time for me. Thanks, Grant; love you, man!

6. *Rich Dad Poor Dad.* This book completely changed the course of my history. My medical school path that I had meticulously planned pre-puberty was thrown into a tailspin my sophomore year of college after I read this book. I realized that economically, medical school was *not* the best decision I could make for my

---

[19]Grant Cardone, *Be Obsessed or Be Average* (New York: Penguin Random House, 2016), 87.
[20]Ibid, 85.

financial well-being. It reaffirmed my innate desire to delay gratification but added the notion of acquiring as many income-producing assets or as much "passive income" as possible. I realized that in order to live the lifestyle I wanted, it would take years of creating value in the world via hard work. My long-term goals would not be reached until after a decade of living off of borrowed money, going through even more school, and jumping through unnecessary hoops, eventually learning how to work. When you read a book and the notions churn in your brain for months and months and you can't ignore the promptings it brings, that usually means it's a pretty good book.

7. *The Millionaire Next Door*. I rethought one of the most expensive purchases of my life and consequently, made one of the best decisions of my life shortly after starting this book. You'll read more about the beautiful car I decided not to buy in an upcoming chapter. Applying the principles in *The Millionaire Next Door* has been, and will continue to be, a differentiating factor between myself and others with a similar income. I plan to accumulate and preserve my success. Now I think about this millionaire mentality that Doctor Stanley so masterfully exposes to his readers on a daily basis. My wife and I talk about those principles all the time. We constantly ask ourselves, "Are we being 'the millionaire next door' with this purchase?" This was more than just a book to me, it was a way of life that I chose to adopt. The book you're reading complements *The Millionaire Next Door* really well; it teaches a lifestyle you have to live not only to accumulate wealth but also to make more money initially. The $300K @ 26 lifestyle is equally tough to adopt, but when the two lifestyles are paired together, you'll have a pretty awesome life.

8. *The Psychology of Selling*. My habit and attitude towards reading was greatly influenced by this book. Brian Tracy urges his readers to read material related to their occupation for thirty to sixty minutes every single day. I'm convinced that one year totally dedicated to internalizing the best books has just as much value as most college degrees. I drive to a ton of appointments for my job, so that's when I listen to books on Audible. My mentality changed from dreading a boring commute to looking forward to forty-minute drives because that means I can really get into the audiobook I'm listening to. Every month, I try to read/listen to anywhere from one to three books that will help develop my skill set and understanding of the world and ultimately, improve my mindset. I've noticed that if I skip listening to books for a few days or heaven forbid, a week, my attitude is in the tank. I start to lose faith in humanity, and I feel like Jim Carrey in *The Truman Show*, thinking everyone who says "no" to me is a part of some grand conspiracy to ruin my life! Reading is like putting on a suit of armor; books fortify your life so when the jabs and the punches come, the blows are weakened. It makes it easier to dust yourself off and get back on track. My good friend, Dave Yates, says, "Negativity has to roll off your back like water off a duck's feathers. The duck can be completely submerged in water, but when it rises to the top again, the water has had no effect on him. No matter how submerged in negative situations you become, it's your choice whether to have duck feathers or dog fur."

Read. Read. Read. It builds up your duck feathers and makes it so the water just rolls off your back.

Don't rely on school to teach you and change you; school actually killed my love of reading. When you're forced to read literature that is boring, seemingly worthless, and irrelevant to life, it turns reading into a dreaded chore. Even worse is when you're forced to write an essay analyzing that useless book. School could be good if it were structured differently. However, what I experienced was a joke, minus a handful of exceptional professors.

The last point I want to touch on with *The Psychology of Selling* is the Pareto Principle; I was first introduced to the notion in this book. It states that 80 percent of your business comes from only 20 percent of your customers. The same goes for managing a sales team: 80 percent of your results come from your top 20 percent of reps, and 80 percent of your results come from 20 percent of your daily actions. I have internalized that concept over the years, gradually adapting my focus toward the key activities of my job that put money in my pocket and ultimately help the most people benefit from my product. If that's true, then hypothetically, you should be able to take a forty-hour work week and condense it down to eight hours. If you make $100,000, then you would take a pay cut down to $80,000. So, by that same logic, if you work that full forty hours focusing only on that 20 percent of most useful tasks, then you should be able to make $400,000. Along those same lines, I hated school and think that I probably could have gained my formal education in a fifth of the time that it took. In my current position, I set my hours, I choose my tasks, and I choose whether to focus on the lucrative 20 percent or the unnecessary 80 percent that deceives you into thinking you're being productive. I'll talk more about this idea in Chapter 16: "Work Smarter, Not Harder."

9. *Outliers*. All literature that I've read by Malcolm Gladwell is fascinating, but this particular book is where I was introduced to the 10,000-hour rule. The rule asserts that it takes about 10,000 hours of deliberate practice to become a master of a particular task, talent, or skill. The impact of this book wasn't so much what I did after reading it, but it's what I didn't do. This book inspired me to stick with the same job, settle down, and work to master my current role. If I ever have thoughts of changing careers or directions or even moving again, that idea is squashed because I will have wasted 10,000 hours learning how to dominate my current position.

When I was a kid, my parents always told me, "You can do anything that you set your mind to." I believed them, but after struggling through tough life lessons, I quickly realized that achieving *anything* is easier said than done. The missing piece to that adage, which I realized by reading this book is, "You can do anything you set your mind to—*if* you spend 10,000 hours working to master it."

10. *The Compound Effect*. Certain books leave you craving more. Repetitive learning and studying is necessary to ingrain the principles taught therein. Along with the publication of those books comes a wealth of follow-up literature, podcasts, Facebook and blog posts, or—in the case of *The Compound Effect*—YouTube videos. The author, Darren Hardy, has a video blog called "Darren Daily," which is a continuous supply of inspiration and motivation to make positive choices so the accumulated tone in your life is positive rather than negative. If you can't tell yet, I love graphs. If my wife would let me, I would frame a picture of this one and hang it over my fireplace because it's just that good:

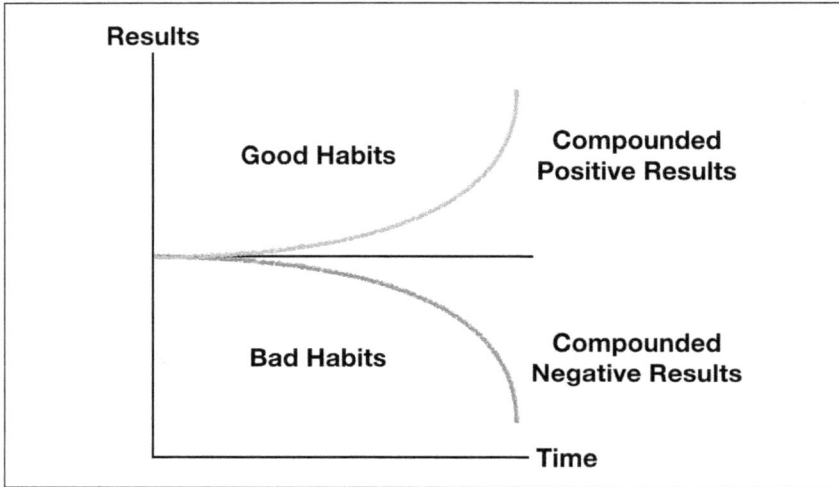

Image 9: The Compound Effect

We become the results of our choices, behaviors, and habits. The results improve or degrade exponentially over time. The end result is an incredibly apparent transformation of either spiraling out of control or launching upward toward unbelievable success. I make choices thinking about how they will compound with time. I try to anticipate the future as if life were a giant game of chess. My brother-in-law Steven always says, "I'm going to do _____ because future Steven will thank me for this." It could be something as simple as taking a bottle of water and chilling it in the fridge. That idea can be applied to everything: marriage, income, cavities, obesity—you name it! You have to think about "future you" and make decisions based on the benefits that will be reaped or sacrificed years down the road, based on the small and simple consistent actions of today.

11. *Rich Dad's Guide to Investing in Gold and Silver.* This book led to my introduction to Goldsilver.com. Since then, I've become obsessed with financial news and financial op-eds. This website has been one of the greatest assets to my financial knowledge. I've been checking this site almost daily for over five years. My understanding of money and how the world operates has been tremendously enhanced because of this resource. The author, Mike Maloney, has become one of my heroes, and it just so happens that he's my father's doppelgänger. Not just their faces are similar, but their mannerisms, laugh, and facial expressions are all identical! As long as they don't double check height, Mike could probably get through airport security with my Dad's ID.

12. *How Will You Measure Your Life?* There are so many gems in this book by Clayton Christensen; it really helped me create a sense of meaning for my work and pursuits. It also helped me reinforce my values and principles, strengthening my resolve to never compromise when it comes to morals. The book says, "It's easier to hold to your principles 100 percent of the time than it is to hold to them 98 percent of the time." My wife and I have listened to this book together three or four times. I feel like it's the book that taught us how to be parents and how to put family first because, as the book says, "If you defer investing your time and energy until you see that you need to, chances are it will already be too late."[21]

This is just a short list of books that had a tremendous impact on my personal growth. These authors took me to this stage of incredible success in my life. This list continues to grow each year.

It's been said that you are what you eat; I believe that you become what you read. Books are food for your brain, so feed it with superfoods and don't stop feeding it! This list is my superfood smoothie that has made me mentally healthier and more confident than I ever thought I could be. My $300K @ 26 lifestyle was shaped and molded by this fantastic literature, along with dozens of other incredible books. The impact those authors had on my life is the same impact I want this book to have in yours.

Free Education

There is value in school, but I don't have a list of college courses I attended that were as influential as the aforementioned literary works. The only reason I finished earning my bachelor's degree was because it was a goal I had set while I was in high school—to finish college, debt free. In order to get a full-ride scholarship, I needed a 4.0 GPA and a 29 on the ACT. I had already received a B in AP US History and earned a 25 on the ACT. The lower your GPA, the higher the ACT score needs to be. It seemed hopeless to earn that scholarship. I went back to my history teacher, Mr. Foxley, and begged him for something to do so I could get my grade up to an A. He conceded and allowed me to rewrite a paper that I had poorly thrown together when I had taken the class originally. I spent about a month working on that paper. I got help from another English professor, who helped me put

---

[21]"Clayton Christensen's "How Will You Measure Your Life?" *Working Knowledge* (blog), Harvard Business School, President & Fellows of Harvard College, May 9, 2012, https://hbswk.hbs.edu/item/clayton-christensens-how-will-you-measure-your-life.

together a cohesive, well-researched paper on the space race. Mr. Foxley read my work, could tell I had put in a significant amount of effort, and changed my grade to that coveted A, which bumped my GPA back up to a 4.0. With that challenge out of the way, I needed to drastically increase my ACT score. I spent the summer and fall semester studying. I spent numerous hours visiting with three different teachers to improve my score in each category. My mother bought an overpriced computer program from a telemarketer that was guaranteed to bump my score up two points; I spent hours upon hours with that resource. As a result of those efforts, I bumped my score up to a 30. From what I've been told, it's pretty difficult to have your score jump up five points. It wasn't easy at all, but the effort was totally worth it! The scholarship I earned was worth about $80,000 over the course of four years. Tuition was only $13,000–$15,000, so I banked the rest to cover all my living expenses. I had worked so hard to get that scholarship, I was motivated to see the fruits of my efforts and earn that college degree everyone told me I needed. I look back on my life thinking about what kind of real-world experience I would have gained had I left school early or not gone at all, and I'm convinced that I would be so much better off now had I just started working. As a salesman, the reason for earning a degree is to be able to "fall back on your education." I'm technically a chemist, and according to Payscale.com, "Earnings for Chemists in the United States come in at around $54K per year on average. In the world of Chemists, total cash compensation can vary between $35K and $84K."[22]

I might sound spoiled, but I've made $84K within three months. I couldn't even imagine ever falling back on my degree. Did I just get the wrong degree? Why did I think chemistry was a good idea? Sales, along with owning and operating a business, is where there is clearly the most opportunity. Sales and business are what makes the world work. With those types of jobs, the potential upside is unlimited, whereas there's a very impenetrable cap on income in just about every other type of job. High risk, high reward. My income is based 100 percent on what I do. If I don't succeed, then I don't make anything, but if I work my bumcheeks off, then I make bank. No college experience that I'm aware of can replace what it feels like to fail at selling or managing a business. No university can give you the same value as real-world work. I think a college education should just be meant for people in very specific degrees. On-the-job training and technical training should definitely be more common in our society. Work ethic is taught in school but only in an academic manner. College was a breeze compared to a summer selling alarms. Like I said before, school felt like vacation after I was beaten down and rejected by what felt like some of the meanest people in the world. I finished my bachelor's degree, but I didn't continue school past that point because it would have cost me more than the value it brought me.

There are more advanced degrees out there that will return way more than my chemistry degree. I had been planning to go to medical school to become a

---

[22]"Chemist Salary," PayScale, PayScale, Inc., accessed 17 October 2017, https://www.payscale.com/research/US/Job=Chemist/Salary.

doctor since I was a little kid. After all, it was and is the family business to be a doctor. My father is a doctor, along with a couple of my uncles. I likewise have three brothers who took that same medical school route. One is a radiologist, another is a neurologist, and the other is an orthodontist. Student loan debt for those specialties typically ranges from $200,000–$600,000. Ouch! They're all still currently in school except the radiologist, who is nine years older than I am and just recently started working in his profession. Comparing myself to that, I basically saved a decade of schooling to get to a similar place. We have a similar amount of debt, except my debt isn't for school, it's my mortgage.

As far as I know, out of all my siblings, no one else achieved this income level or hit these huge goals when they were my age. We were all raised by the same parents. What was the difference with me? My choice to pursue an alternative education has made me an outlier in my family. Outliers exist because they take the less traveled paths. They seek learning outside of the mainstream methods. They don't conform. They don't comply. They don't let themselves be shepherded through life like dispensable cogs. They relentlessly carve their own way to the top of the charts and beyond.

7 Run Away from Home ASAP and Burn the Boats!

Building Character

I recently read an article from NPR titled, "For First Time in 130 Years, More Young Adults Live With Parents Than With Partners." It would seem that the financial crisis of 2008 had a huge negative impact on the independence and self-sufficiency of my generation. I feel like parents have become a crutch, a safety net that doesn't let millennials fail forward into success. Can we not cook our own food or do our own laundry? I absolutely love my parents, but there's no way I could live with them and be where I am today financially, emotionally, or mentally. It would be too easy to coast through life, nonchalantly trying to figure out what I wanted to do rather than getting my hands dirty and just doing what I need to.

Whether it was intentional or not, I'm grateful that my parents started kicking me out of their house when I turned sixteen. We moved from what my elementary school friends considered a mansion in Florida to a single-wide trailer in the middle-of-nowhere Wyoming. On the eastern side of that trailer, where the early morning sun pierced my teenage eyes on a daily basis, there was an addition hanging on for dear life, half-attached to the main body of that mobile home. I clearly recall a six-inch gap under the stairs that connected that room to the main part of the house. The ground had shifted, pulling the trailer and the addition apart. You could see the outside world, and in the wintertime, it felt as though you *were* outside. The first time my wife came to meet my family, she stayed in that room and distinctly remembers it smelling like dead mice. The only door that room had for my sentence was a bedsheet, apart from the door leading outside, which allowed for barely an ounce of privacy. In the winter, the steps to the front door would freeze and raise up high enough that they were rendered unusable, which meant that the back door in my room became the only usable door. I remember the sounds and feelings so vividly: "Stomp, stomp, stomp, stomp, squeaky door opens, blast of -20-degree air, door slams, stomp, stomp . . . " If they forgot something: "Stomp, stomp, squeaky door opens and slams with a blast of cold air, stomp, stomp, stomp, stomp, stomp, stomp, someone yells, 'Where are my keys?' Stomp, stomp, door opens and slams with cold air and squeaks, stomp, stomp . . ." And then another person or two might come out behind them with the same cadence. I hated Saturday mornings.

Did I resent my parents for moving from a 5,000-square-foot house in Florida where I basically had my own massive private wing of the house to live in, to giving me my own half-eaten wing hanging off the side of a trailer? Maybe a little . . .

My dad always liked to say things like: "One day, if you finish college, go to medical school, and then practice medicine as a doctor for twenty years, maybe you, too, can buy your own single-wide trailer." Have you ever read the *Calvin and Hobbes* comic books? Calvin's father was famous for saying miserable experiences "build character."

That was basically my experience growing up.

My room in that trailer built some serious character. I knew that I never wanted to live in a trailer again. It was a home built with the cheapest materials, constantly falling apart, meant to become a slum. Have you ever heard of someone in the single-wide trailer home renovation business? No one fixes trailers; you can probably buy a brand-new one for less than the cost to renovate!

How I Met Your Mother

My wife, Aubree, and I met doing missionary work for our church. There's a training center in Provo, Utah, where you learn how to teach, maybe learn how to give tours, and you also might be required to learn conversational basics of a foreign language in only ten weeks. We met briefly in that setting, exchanged our addresses, and then we went our separate ways to opposite sides of the country. We wrote letters every week for two years; we still have those letters, and they're one of our most prized possessions. We also sent a recording device back and forth for a year and a half of that time. Missionary rules are strict; you can't make phone calls home except on Christmas and Mother's Day, and that phone call is usually limited only to your immediate family, and I think we had a time limit, like thirty to sixty minutes. There was also no TV or movies, no physical contact with the opposite sex other than a handshake, and you had to stay within a certain geographic boundary that was usually less than a ten mile radius. (As I'm writing this, I realize it kind of sounds like I was actually in prison in somewhere crazy like Siberia or Guantanamo. I promise I wasn't. I really was on a mission, and it really was an amazing experience.) Anyway, my then-future-wife and I wrote for that entire time.

She came home six months before I did, had a couple of boyfriends during that time, and somehow waited for me to come home before she got too serious with anyone else. She waited even though she was a hot commodity and in super high demand! Five days after I came home from my mission, I hitched a ride with my brother to the Salt Lake City airport. The car broke down in the middle of the desert, but I miraculously made it in time. I flew out to Sacramento, where Aubree picked me up at the airport. We had our first kiss within minutes of seeing each other. We went to her sister's house for a welcome home/engagement party for us. After eight hectic weeks, which included calling off the ceremony twice, we were married.

Empathize with my parents for a second: for two years, they only got to speak with me for an hour or two, and not even a week had passed after I returned home before I had disappeared to marry a girl they had no clue even existed. Right before the wedding, my bride-to-be met me in Nevada and whisked me off into the sunset toward our happily ever after. I started my third semester of college a week after our marriage.

What this ultimately did for us is force us out of our parents' houses. We weren't going to live with either of our families after getting married. No way! (Although, it might've been fun living in the wing off the trailer together—free birth control!) We were suddenly forced to become adults. We declared our independence and consequently, were in a position that necessitated learning personal responsibility and self-sufficiency. Decisions sure are different when you're not only free but also alone. I'm sure the US had very similar growing pains after declaring independence from Great Britain. Like the United States, my wife and I have had our share of civil wars and issues to work through. Despite disputes here and there, I'm extremely happy with my decision to elope with her and in turn, choose to fight our way through life's battles as partners and best friends.

Now that I have my own kids, my perspective on this idea is evolving. I'm going to miss my daughters like crazy when they eventually follow suit; I dread that day when they may choose to emulate my exodus and run away from home. Could they grow to their full potential if they stayed at home with the safety net we provide? My greatest desire is their happiness; I know that a certain level of independence and space will be necessary, although not the easiest thing to accept as a parent.

Burn the Boats

If there's always a safety net knowing that your parents will take care of you, you'll never act with complete confidence in your own talents and abilities. I still remember one of the very first training videos I ever saw when I started working for Vivint. It was a video intended to hype you up and get you stoked for the summer selling season. The video starred a former New England Patriots defensive end named Setema Gali; he spoke with such boldness and determination that his message has resonated with me ever since. In the video, he talked about Hernán Cortés and his strategy to conquer the Mayan Empire.

An excerpt from Burningboats.com illustrates the tale perfectly and references a number of other similar situations:

> It was the year 1519 and Hernán Cortés, with some 600 Spaniards, 16 or so horses and 11 boats, had landed on a vast inland plateau called, Mexico.
>
> The Spanish conquistador and his men were about to embark on a conquest of an empire that hoarded some of the world's greatest treasure. Gold, silver and precious Aztec jewels were just some of what this treasure had to offer anyone who succeeded in their quest to obtain it.
>
> But, with only 600 men — none of whom had encumbered themselves with protective armour — conquering an empire so extensive in its territories could only be undertaken by a man with a death wish.
>
> This daring undertaking was made even more insurmountable by the fact that for more than 600 years, conquerors with far more resources at their disposal who attempted to colonize the Yucatan Peninsula, never succeeded. Hernán Cortés was well-aware of this fact. And it was for this reason, that he took a different approach when he landed on the land of the Mayans. Instead of charging through cities and forcing his men into immediate battle, Hernán Cortés stayed on the beach and awoke the souls of his men with melodious cadences — in the form of emblazoned speeches.
>
> His speeches were ingeniously designed to urge on the spirit of adventure and invoke the thirst of lifetimes of fortune amongst his troops. His orations bore fruit, for what was supposedly a military exploit, now bore the appearance of extravagant romance in the imaginations of Cortés' troops.
>
> But, ironically, it would only just be 3 words which Cortés murmured, that would change the history of the New World. As they marched inland to face their enemies, Cortés ordered, "**Burn the boats**."

It was a decision that should have backfired. For if Cortés and his men were on the brink of defeat, there wasn't an exit strategy in place to save their lives. Remarkably though, the command to burn the boats had an opposite effect on his men because now, they were left with only 2 choices — die, or ensure victory. And fight they did.

We know today, how Cortés' decision to burn his boats panned out. Hernán Cortés became the first man in 600 years to successfully conquer Mexico.

Though historians still dispute the veracity of Hernán Cortés burning his boats, it's doubtless that Cortés did destroy his boats. But he wasn't the first man to make such a bold, strategic decision to ensure victory.

About a thousand years before, the world's greatest empire builder, Alexander the Great burned his boats upon arrival on the shores of Persia. By burning his boats, Alexander committed his men to victory over the Persians, who far outnumbered the Greeks in great numbers. Furthermore, Persia then also had the distinction of having the most powerful naval fleet in the world. Considering what Alexander was facing, the decision to destroy the Greeks' only hope of retreat was an extraordinary one. Nonetheless, it proved to be the correct one.

Our history books also boast of other fearsome Greek commanders who executed the same strategy to guarantee victory. Taric el Tuerto, otherwise known as Tariq ibn Ziyad, the general who conquered Hispania in 711, burned his boats when fighting the Spaniards, as he too had a valid reason to do so — his army was outnumbered 5:1.

Was this act of burning the boats a mock dramatization of bravery, or a cleverly constructed strategy? In Sun Tzu's *The Art of War*, it brings to light the logic behind the decisions of history's greatest conquerors to burn their boats at the risk of being killed in enemy hands. It was simply to eradicate any notion of retreat from the minds of their troops and commit themselves unwaveringly to the cause — Victory. Defeat wasn't an option at all.[23]

Those three words, "Burn the boats" have such power if applied to your unique situation. Family support can be good, but it can also be distracting, facilitate dependency, create a crutch, and limit your growth. In this day and age, we're surrounded by millennials who are dependent primarily on their parents for food, clothing, housing, tuition, textbooks, health insurance, dental insurance, vision insurance, car insurance, renter's insurance, car payment, gas money, phone

[23]"About BurningBoats.com," Kevin-Mikhail Mansour Singarayar, BurningBoats, accessed 17 October 2017, http://burningboats.com/about-burningboatscom/.

bills, electronic toys—everything! If they had no ship to run back to or no way to run away from a fight, from a challenge, or from obstacles in their way, how would that change their confidence? How would it change their consumption habits and how would they adapt in order to afford what they currently enjoy for free?

Once I ran away, I couldn't ask for a thing from my parents; I tore down my safety net, and as a result, I *had* to be successful because it felt like there was nothing and no one there to catch me. Have I gone to counseling because it was one of the toughest things I've ever done in my life? Yep, at least half a dozen sessions trying to cope with it. Was the freedom worth the stress? Was the newfound confidence worth the pain and heartache? Was the long-term success worth going through that initial sadness? Absolutely. Like Taric el Tuerto, I've felt out-numbered five to one, with the odds stacked against me achieving any level of success. The odds have definitely been against me earning more or achieving more than 99 percent of people my age. With that being said, it's important to note that the work and effort required to succeed is not lessened if you burn your ships. However, your mentality adapts to the circumstances and your focus be-comes clearer because you're cornered and have no escape; you force yourself into having no choice other than victory. Innate survival instincts kick in at that point, and that's when the magic happens.

Now I don't want this chapter to be mistaken as me saying that I dislike my par-ents or that I'm in any way ungrateful to them. Their wisdom and guidance was invaluable to me, and ultimately, their parenting style helped me leave the nest. My father and mother are my heroes; they instilled in me many of the values and ideas in this book. I feel like my parents may have run away from home just like I did. If you never leave your comfort zone, you can never truly achieve your potential. There's so much to be gained by declaring independence. Had the United States never declared independence, would the world have smart-phones, microwaves, chocolate chip cookies, baseball, or Netflix? Maybe. Just as Europe led the world out of the Dark Ages and into the Renaissance, the US led the world out of the Industrial Age and into the Information Age. In both cas-es, there was a sudden freedom granted to the people. The US government sud-denly became by the people, for the people, and of the people. Self-governance was an incredible new concept that led the world in a direction of innovation and excellence. Not only did the early American pilgrims and colonists "burn their boats" figuratively, but they also literally burned the boats of their over-involved English motherland. A whole country was founded by a group of people who ran away from home. I've always loved the third verse of "America the Beautiful":

O beautiful for heroes proved
In liberating strife,
Who more than self their country loved
And mercy more than life!
America! America!
May God thy gold refine,
Till all success be nobleness,
And every gain divine![24]

Burning your boats is a beautiful metaphor for committing to your cause, demonstrating extreme ownership, and deciding that you will either achieve your goal or die. That phrase always gives me the chills: "Who more than self their country loved and mercy more than life."

---

[24]"America the Beautiful," by Katharine Lee Bates and Samuel A. Ward, 1911.

8 Goals

My wife will tell you that she married me because she saw how goal oriented I was. I always had my eyes set on being the best at whatever I did. I rarely was the best at anything, but I continued to aim for the top spot regardless of past failure.

In 2014, I was in school for the first half of the year; I ended the year making $90,000, which for my age, puts me in the 97th percentile. In 2015, I made $180,000, which put me well into the 99th percentile. Then in 2016, I made right around $300,000. All these numbers fell short of the goals that I set for myself each year:

> 2014: $100k
> 2015: $200k
> 2016: $350k

I've fallen short by 10–15 percent the last three years in a row. At the time, those goals were bigger than anything I had believed was possible. I landed within 10-15 percent of absolutely massive goals each year! Just getting close to hitting each of those was a remarkable achievement that completely reshaped how I view the world.

At the beginning of each year, I write down my income goal and keep it on an index card in my wallet as a consistent reminder. Look up Earl Nightingale's *The Strangest Secret*. If you haven't listened to it before, put this book down and listen to it. It'll be one of the most worthwhile half hours of your life if you internalize and apply what he says. I got the idea to write my goal on the note card from that recording. As I mentioned in Chapter 1, Nightingale also helped mold my definition of success as "the progressive realization of a worthy goal or ideal."[25]

The purpose of this chapter is to help you set goals immediately after you finish reading it. I want you to put yourself on the track toward true success—starting today. I have a few valuable insights on setting worthy goals and a few easily implementable tips for achieving them. This is an important chapter to pay close attention to. Goals are, without a doubt, the lifeblood of the $300K @ 26 lifestyle.

Pharaoh's Dream and Holy Causes

In the Bible, the book of Genesis tells the story of a prophetic dream, or vision, that has been applicable to my life.

> And it came to pass at the end of two full years, that Pharaoh dreamed: and, behold, he stood by the river. And, behold, there came up out of the river seven well favoured kine and fatfleshed; and they fed in a meadow. And, behold, seven other kine came up after them out of the river, ill favoured and leanfleshed; and stood by the other kine upon the brink of the river. And the ill favoured and leanfleshed kine did eat up the seven well favoured and fat kine. So Pharaoh awoke.[26]

Image 10: Pharoah's Dream

---

[25]Earl Nightingale, "Success: A Worthy Destination," Nightingale, Nightingale-Conant Corporation, accessed 17 October 2017, http://www.nightingale.com/articles/success-a-worthy-destination/.
[26]Gen. 41:1–4

Chapter 8: Goals

One of my mentors, Casey Baugh, gave a training to our leadership group using this example from the Bible. My biggest takeaway was that I need to have extreme gratitude and care for my current opportunity. I've been able to make a ridiculous amount of money in a very short period of time. It would be so easy to live paycheck to paycheck, spending all my extra money on luxuries, trinkets, and doodads. I've found that there's a better way to live. Adopting the Egyptian attitude after Pharaoh had that vision is congruent with long-term success. It's so important to treat the present as if you only have seven years of fat and healthy cows, or fortune and success, in anticipation of seven years of skinny cows, or recession and hardship. What did the Egyptians do when they received the interpretation of Pharaoh's dream? They got to work! They set huge goals; they knew that every year they worked, they needed to make at least twice what they needed for the entire year. They knew that for every day's worth of plentiful grain they harvested, there would be another day of famine in the not-too-distant future. They stockpiled the extra and didn't squander their time. During the seven years of famine, Egypt had enough extra grain to sell to other countries who hadn't prepared themselves appropriately for the shortage. As a result, they became a wealthy and powerful empire.

Setting and achieving big goals now puts you in a position of leverage; it allows you to write the rules and set terms in the future. The more financially secure you become compared to those around you, the smaller investment you will need to have in order to yield the biggest returns. The fulcrum of fortune is shifted in your favor. This reminds me of the board game, *The Settlers of Catan*. In the game, you produce resources every time you roll the dice, but you can trade them with the other players in the game to get what you need in order to buy new buildings and roads. When people are desperate for scarce resources, you can ask the other players to trade for just about anything and you'll get it. It feels good to be on the side with leverage. It sucks to be on the desperate side of the equation, begging for necessities.

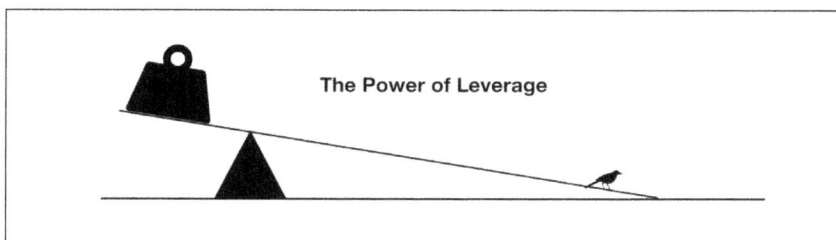

Image 11: The Fulcrum of Fortune

Throughout life, if a season of great opportunity and fortune is squandered, someone else who worked harder and saved their excess will be the one with leverage over you. It doesn't feel great to be at the mercy of others. I personally like being in control. I prefer to *choose* my destiny, rather than be forced into a corner by my needs.

Had the people of Egypt not prepared for the famine, the sickly cows would have eaten the fat cows. Meaning that any progress or any economic expansion on Egypt's part would have been completely wiped out by a recession that came with the famine. Working for seven years only to have all the progress disappear would have been a pretty miserable experience. Don't squander the present! Have urgency! Treat every year like it's the last good harvest you'll ever see. Give due respect to the incredible opportunities that surround us; if you live on the same Earth I do, then I know there are limitless ways to earn a living; there are infinite ways to gain an education, and success is right around the corner for those willing to claim it.

My goal each year has been to earn double what I need. The attitude needed to set a successful goal and follow through with it is: "This opportunity could be gone tomorrow, I need to make the most of it while it lasts." Why not aim to reach the upper limits of your potential while things are going well? I would rather set big goals in a period of prosperity than in a period of frugality and poverty. My current successes will hopefully compensate for my future struggles if I can earn more than I need today.

Adopting this attitude improves performance more than you can imagine. This new attitude includes a shift in the deeper purpose for working at all. I'm not necessarily working for materialistic goods. I'm not working for a sports car or a boat or a $10,000 watch. Those things might be purchased one day, but for now, the good fortune needs to be received with thanksgiving. It needs to be preserved and protected, accumulated, and appreciated. The money I make now is sacred to me and to my family. My work today will feed my children for years to come and provide them with an education that will set them up for success. This work represents future joy, peace, and security for my family. I work to earn money for these holy causes. The health and happiness of my family is worth more than any material item.

I suggest maxing out retirement contributions as soon as you can. The younger you are, the better. Invest in your businesses, other businesses, yourself, your spouse, and your children. Make a budget and include rainy-day money; those days will surely come. Give to charity, at least 10 percent of what you make. Just give it away. You appreciate what you keep more when you give a significant portion away. Is that a holy cause? A reason to work harder to make more money? To make more money just so you can give more away? Is it your dream to run or fund a specific charity organization? To raise millions of dollars for noble causes? Do you want to make a lasting difference in the world by helping out hundreds and thousands of individuals who are struggling, trapped in a forlorn life? Would it give you meaning and joy to help those who sadly find themselves in a less fortunate and downtrodden plight? Helping those in need fills the soul and gives purpose. Sure, self-gratification is fun occasionally, but that heartwarming feeling of overall wellbeing and wholeness is the most pronounced when serving and lifting others.

My biggest holy cause over the last few years has been to buy a home. Not just a house—a home. My goal was to have a place where I could raise my family and provide them with safety, stability, privacy, nature, comfort, learning, health, joy, peace, unity, creativity, fun, spirituality, love, support, encouragement, beauty, quiet, warmth, acceptance, individuality, laughter, and a pure life. My mother is from the small Central American country, Costa Rica. In Costa Rica, they have a saying that seems to be appropriately used in almost every sentence you can think of. The saying is, "*Pura vida*" or "Pure life." *Pura vida* is more than just a saying or a salutation; it's a lifestyle that represents the culture's love for life, nature, and family. It could mean, "I'm living the dream," or, "No matter how bad things get, life is still pretty good and could always be worse." Life is so different down in Costa Rica; much of the population is living a truly pure, unadulterated, non-materialistic, and simple life. My holy cause has been to create a space, an environment, a home where my family could experience this paradisiacal *pura vida* on a daily basis. I can say with absolute certainty that the infinite value of having a *home* greatly exceeds the cost and work required to buy a house.

Create the Path of Least Resistance

I already told you in Chapter 3 to take the path of most resistance. Now I'm telling you to create the path of least resistance in order to achieve your goals. Let me explain.

Take fitness goals as an example. Fitness goals are much easier to achieve if you don't have to think or give much effort to start your workout. How long will your workout routine last if you daily encounter the following: it's snowing outside; you have to find your keys, socks, tennis shoes, workout clothes, a bottle of water, and a protein bar; you have to get dressed, get in your car, drive thirty minutes, and then check in at a gym so you can finally begin the actual workout. After the workout, you then still have to drive back home, shower, re-deodorize, and change clothes again. I'm exhausted just thinking about that whole process. I hate New Year's resolutions because for most people, the changes only last for a couple weeks and then quickly die off and they regress back to old habits. People go way out of their way and set up workout plans that change their routine drastically and as a result, are not successful.

My company started a fitness competition this year. I've been wanting to start a workout routine, and this gave me an excuse to start. I bought a jump rope, some brand-new tennis shoes, and a dozen pairs of socks. I keep the socks and shoes right by the jump rope in the entryway to my house. This is now where I jump rope. When I walk by that set up, it's almost easier for me to start working out than any other activity. Fitness and nutrition often go hand in hand; for this reason, I keep my Vitamix on our kitchen countertop, ready to be used. We also cut up and froze a bunch of fruit and vegetables in zip-bags that we use for post-workout protein smoothies.

In his incredible book, *The 10x Rule,* Grant Cardone talks about how he thinks it's ridiculous how people tell you to hold back and set "realistic" goals. He says we need to set goals that are ten times bigger than what we want or need. I agree that goals should be set way higher than what we think is possible, but then, it's critical that our actions and preparation reflect the intensity of those goals. We need to make it realistic to achieve those goals. We need to make it easier to achieve the goals than to not achieve them. If you want to cut back on eating candy, don't put crispy M&Ms in a fancy glass cup right in the middle of the kitchen—you'll take a handful of them every time you walk by. If you want to cut back on eating ice cream, a suggestion I have is this: in the middle of winter, store the Ben & Jerry's in a freezer in your garage. Maybe have the freezer be behind an enormous pile of empty Amazon boxes and broken glass from a mirror that needs to be thrown away. Maybe also keep a bunch of junk on top of the lid of the freezer so it isn't very convenient to open. Like me, I guarantee you'll be reluctant to go out there no matter what flavor ice cream you have.

Fitness and nutrition are basic examples. An even tougher application of this principle is in your work ethic. How can you make it the path of least resistance to go do more cold calling or account management as a sales rep? Here are a few things that have made it easier for me to succeed:

1. My car is wrapped with my company name and logo. There's a distinct tone when I'm driving that car: I'm always working when I drive it. It feels like I'm driving a billboard, and it feels like everyone is always looking at me. Why not talk to someone about my product? Wrapping the car was the best $250 investment I ever made.
2. In my job, the toughest part of each day is getting out of the car to walk up to strangers' doors. To combat that challenge, I drive a car that isn't super comfortable. There's nothing special about the seats, no cushy leather, no seat heaters, no extra nothing. To top it off, I'm a little taller than six feet, and I drive a tiny Smart Car; I feel like Mr. Incredible, especially if I have a passenger. That claustrophobia and discomfort is relieved when I get out of that miserable car. The less time I spend in my car, the more time I spend with customers, creating and closing business.
3. I hired a company for a month or two to cold-call people in my area and set sales appointments for me. This made it so I *had* to get out of my house and I *had* to go out and work. If I didn't go to work, then I was missing out on an opportunity. It literally felt easier for me to go to those appointments than to sit around at home.
4. Have my phone or iPad with me all the time. My phone gives me access to manage my schedule, respond to my emails, communicate with my

sales reps, and push forward and follow up on all my customers' accounts. It's easy to work when I have access to those devices.

5. Book appointments a week in advance. I usually have a pretty full week planned, and again, having those appointments preset makes it easier to work than to not work. It's just like having my jump rope staring at me every time I walk by the entryway to my house.

6. Have specific hours that I *always* work. Because I always work during that time, it feels weird if I ever try to take that time off. The hours of 3–6 pm are non-negotiable in my mind. I will be working or in the hospital, and even then, I might be trying to sell something to the staff. This one meshes well with Chapter 15 when I talk about discipline.

7. Resolve my excuses before they come up. The best example I can think of is hunger. When I'm out working and I get hungry, it would be so easy to call it quits and go home to eat lunch or dinner. Spending time at home midday can be a work ethic black hole from whence you never return. Taking a protein bar that tastes good, satisfies my hunger, and quickly gives me energy resolves that problem in seconds. That food has to be in my car, though, and easily accessible; otherwise, it's not the path of least resistance.

8. Set appointments at the beginning of the day and at the end of the day. If someone is super flexible with their time, I set an appointment for 1 pm or 7 pm. This gets me out of my house at a reasonable hour for my profession or keeps me out later than I would typically want to. If I start early in the day, why not work until dark? If I have an appointment at night, then I figure I might as well work until then. Again, it's easier to work than to not work when I do this. I'm not going to go home in the middle of the day if I have a 1 pm and a 7 pm appointment. If I go home, I'll have to use more emotional energy to leave home again. It's easier to stay in my area and prospect.

9. Have a book downloaded that I'm excited to listen to in my car. I love listening to audiobooks, but the only time I really get to listen to them is while I'm driving. I have to drive to go to work. It's become a rewarding treat for me to go to work. I get excited and think, "Alright, I get to listen to my book!" The driving portion of my work time has become a therapeutic pastime that stimulates my brain, reenergizes my mentality, and re-centers my life. I look forward to that period of renewal. It's been a key path of least resistance.

Set Goals That Bring Joy and Motivation

Einstein has been credited for saying, "Everybody is a genius. But if you judge a fish by its ability to climb a tree, it will live its whole life believing that it is stupid." My wife and I have many similar interests, but we have many interests that are completely different. About the same time I started writing this book, my wife started playing a game on her iPhone called *Super Mario Run*. We were both equally obsessed with these tasks. It took her about the same length of time to finish all the levels of that game that it took me to write the first half of this book. We were both so obsessed that we may have spent hours on the toilet, toiling to accomplish our individual goals. We both were so happy and fulfilled as we were achieving these goals. She was fighting to beat Bowser in a game that reminded her of her childhood, and I was pouring my soul into this book.

After she completed every level in that game, she poured that same obsession into a business selling lipstick. She was extremely passionate about sharing it with everyone she talked to because she personally wore it every single day and absolutely loved the product.

I find it tough to transfer enthusiasm about a product that I would never use. My goals are MY goals. Don't set goals that other people want for you. Be yourself and enjoy life! My wife will excel at tons of tasks that I never will and vice versa.

Steve Jobs said, "The only way to be truly satisfied is to do what you believe is great work. And the only way to do great work is to love what you do. If you haven't found it yet, keep looking. Don't settle. As with all matters of the heart, you'll know when you find it."[27]

Continuing on that same theme, each time after my wife gave birth to one of our three daughters, she set the goal to compete in a beauty pageant that includes strutting her stuff in a bathing suit on stage, often in front of hundreds of people. Her goal each time has been to get back to her pre-pregnancy weight and physique. She's done so well every single time! As a result, I think she's gotten more attractive with each consecutive pregnancy. She sets that goal to become more active in order to avoid postpartum anxiety and depression; also, she wants to do something for herself. Can you blame her? With each birth, she had just spent nine months either throwing up with morning sickness or waddling with a watermelon in her belly resting right on her bladder.

Pageants are pretty awesome experiences if they're done right. In the time leading up to the competition, the participants are actively looking for service projects and things they can do to help improve the community around them. They make a positive, lasting difference for a wide range of people in need. They provide a positive role model for youth who may not have good influences in their lives. Preparation for the interviews has led my wife to read dozens of self-help books with the intent to grow her character and develop a more friendly, helping personality. After they compete, they receive recognition for their accomplishments, personality, and for their beauty. Think what you may about pageants, but for all the criticism, there is just as much, if not more, of a positive impact on the people who have proper intentions.

---

[27]Steve Jobs, "'You've got to find what you love,' Jobs says" (speech, Stanford University, June 12, 2005), Stanford News, http://news.stanford.edu/2005/06/14/jobs-061505/.

When you set goals, you have to make sure the goals you set will truly motivate *you* specifically. Setting a goal to make a ton of money is great, but it should be coupled with something that will motivate you. My immediate superior often refers to the research done in the 1960s by a psychologist named Frederick Herzberg. He developed what's called the Two-Factor Theory:

Two-factor theory distinguishes between:

- **Motivators** (e.g., challenging work, recognition for one's achievement, responsibility, opportunity to do something meaningful, involvement in decision making, sense of importance to an organization) that give positive satisfaction, arising from intrinsic conditions of the job itself, such as recognition, achievement, or personal growth, and

- **Hygiene factors** (e.g., status, job security, salary, fringe benefits, work conditions, good pay, paid insurance, vacations) that do not give positive satisfaction or lead to higher motivation, though dissatisfaction results from their absence. The term "hygiene" is used in the sense that these are maintenance factors. These are extrinsic to the work itself, and include aspects such as company policies, supervisory practices, or wages/salary. Herzberg often referred to hygiene factors as "KITA" factors, which is an acronym for "kick in the ass", the process of providing incentives or threat of punishment to make someone do something.[28]

Basically, there are two ways your motivation can go, up or down. How you work to achieve your goals will determine which way you go.

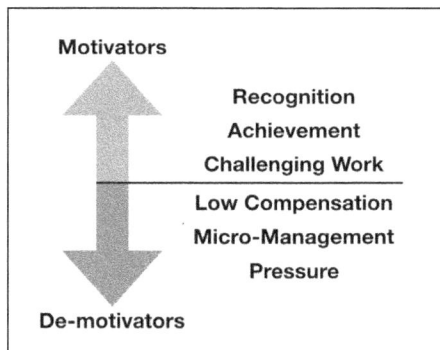

Image 12: Money Employee Motivation

[28]"Two-factor theory," Wikipedia, Wikimedia Foundation, last modified 13 September 2017, 13:22, https://en.wikipedia.org/wiki/Two-factor_theory.

So, with the pageant example, my wife had the goal to lose her baby weight, but she also coupled that with preparation to compete in a pageant. All the motivators are present in this example, and there are virtually no de-motivators. She wasn't getting paid because the work she does is all for charity. She has job security because no one would kick her out of the pageant, and if she wins, she reigns for a year. All her hygiene factors are taken care of in this example; that's why she returns to compete time after time. Throughout the months of preparation, she experienced and looked forward to an increase in responsibility, achievement, recognition, challenging work, personal growth, and advancement.

In Chapter 5, I talked about your circle of influence. That circle of five people you spend most of your time with can make or break your motivation. Being surrounded by people who underpay you or threaten to fire you every other day, harass you, or micromanage you will make you want to quit your job. If instead, your circle of influence knows how to use true motivators, pushing you to grow and advance and then recognizing that progress, it will make a world of difference. I want to reiterate that some relationships are toxic. It could be a coworker or even a family member. You know the people I'm talking about. The ones who make you just feel worse after you've been around them. Leave them. Drop them. Don't let them hold you back. Don't let them rob you of motivation. I have to reevaluate and remove myself of toxic influences on a regular basis.

Those motivators are things that will bring lasting joy. The hygiene factors are fleeting and temporal. Money isn't the target, it's a perk that comes as you're working toward those motivating factors that are intrinsic to the nature of your occupation.

Couple your tough goals with a motivating/joy-inducing goal or reward, and the probability of success increases exponentially. Basically, give yourself a prize for accomplishing a challenge. I've seen the success from doing this on many different occasions throughout my life. Here are a few examples:

1. **Goal:** Earn a full ride scholarship to college.
   Prize: I would then have enough extra money to buy a motorcycle. I can't tell you how much fun that motorcycle was. Going zero to sixty in 3.04 seconds never gets old. It feels like you threw on a helmet and strapped yourself to a rogue missile. When I first got it, I would get on and off the highway just so I could pop wheelies and go from a dead stop to 100 mph before I even got on the highway. Talk about an ultimate sense of freedom and power. It really gets to your head; you start to feel invincible on those glorious machines

2. **Goal:** Finish college.
   Prize: My self-reasoning was that with my degree, I could then earn enough money to get LASIK. No regrets: I would get LASIK again, no questions asked. I hated looking for my glasses all the time! Now I'm looking for eyedrops all the time, but at least I can see where I'm looking.

3. **Goal:** Hit my income goal so I would get promoted within a year of working for my company.
   Prize: Advancement is a huge part of personal satisfaction. Promotions typically involve every single one of the motivators.

When my wife was meeting with a personal trainer, going to kickboxing classes, and going on jogs with a stroller, she wasn't thinking about her cardiovascular health. She was thinking about how she would look on stage. She was thinking about how good she would look in a swimsuit. The good health was a byproduct of a worthy goal. When I was in college, I wasn't necessarily thinking about how useful it would be for my career to learn advanced Spanish grammar. I clearly remember thinking, "If I can just get through this class, I can reward myself with LASIK one day." The language skills were a byproduct of my real motivation.

Again, my goals are not my wife's goals and vice versa. Making a ton of money in order to buy an expensive dress to compete in a pageant just doesn't do it for me. A new goal that I recently made is to buy an apartment building. I spent about five minutes online and found a $2,000,000, thirty-unit building with a 95 percent occupancy rate. That gets me excited! I think about owning that thing, and I get these weird happy chills and start smiling. To get to that point where I can put a down payment on something that size, I probably need between $400-$600K. Making money and saving money toward that goal makes the idea of tough work seem totally worth it.

"A goal is a dream with a deadline." —Napoleon Hill

"An unwritten goal is merely a wish." —Unknown Author

"Only 3 percent of adults have clear, written, specific, measurable, time-bounded goals, and by every statistic, they accomplish ten times as much as people with no goals at all. Why is it then that most people have no goals?" —Brian Tracy[29]

If you want to accomplish something that very few people achieve, you have to be willing to do the things that no one else is willing to do. Only 3 percent of people write their goals in a productive manner. What's stopping you from doing the same?

Some of the best advice I ever received was from a VP in my company named Casey Baugh. He did a training with a small group of salesmen late one night in Lake Charles, Louisiana, where I was selling alarms. Casey told us that one of the most important things he turned into a habit was writing in a goal book every Sunday. He did an exercise with us where he asked us to write, "What would I do if I knew I couldn't fail?" He then asked us to write down our most intimate desires and dreams. My heart and soul poured onto the page as I wrote down

---

[29]Brian Tracy, "Setting Goals and Objectives: 5 Myths," Brian Tracy International, accessed 17 October 2017, https://www.briantracy.com/blog/general/setting-goals-and-objectives-5-myths/.

my most intimate dreams. He then asked us to put a number next to every single one of those dreams. The number was either a one, three, five, or ten. That number represented how many years it would take to achieve that goal. That was almost three years ago. That list suddenly transformed from simply a list of wishes into goals after I wrote them down and assigned a deadline. I'd like to share a few of those dreams that I wrote down on that memorable late rainy night:

2. Become a manager for Vivint Solar: 3
8. Be perfectly honest and be known for it: 1
11. Go sky diving: 5
14. Buy a house: 3
18. Write a book: 5
25. Get LASIK: 1
31. Develop a studious, always reading, always improving habit: 1
33. Earn $200,000 within one year of graduating from college: 1

I accomplished every single one of these goals, and most were realized ahead of schedule. Only LASIK was delayed because I moved across the country right after my first evaluation; otherwise, it would have been within that year. I did a similar exercise in my sales class my last semester of college, and it's uncanny to look back and see how my life has turned out exactly the way I planned it would, with my "clear, written, specific, measurable, time-bounded goals." In retrospect, it feels like there is literally some kind of magic that happens when you write down a goal in this manner. You suddenly become accountable to yourself; then it's as if you've planned your future just like you would plan a vacation or a birthday party. I wrote down the details of my future and then worked to make those details come to pass. My mind was focused and fine-tuned toward making it happen.

For the past three years, I've written my income goal down on an index card. I keep that index card in my wallet so I am reminded of that goal at all times. I physically carry my written goal everywhere I go, and consequently, I mentally carry that goal with me everywhere. The Law of Attraction is a very real principle. You literally attract what you think about. Shawn Achor, the author of *The Happiness Advantage*, has said:

> We can now peer behind the curtain to see what the brain is doing. The brain can process 40 bits of information per second. But it receives 11-million bits of information per second. What we attend to first becomes our reality, which means we often can't scan the world for that which is more meaningful. What this means is scientifically, happiness is a choice for the individual. We can create the happiness advantage, our ability to use our knowledge and technical skills to their highest degree.[30]

---

[30]"CFOs Told They Can Still Worry, But Real Benefit Is in Happiness," CUtoday.info, CUtoday, accessed 17 October 2017, https://www.cutoday.info/THE-feature/CFOs-Told-They-Can-Still-Worry-But-Real-Benefit-is-in-Happiness.

When goals are written, the "bits of information" in the world around us are filtered, and we consciously and subconsciously choose to process the forty out of eleven million bits that come our way every second. As Zig Ziglar said, "The great majority of people are 'wandering generalities' rather than 'meaningful specifics'. The fact is that you can't hit a target that you can't see. If you don't know where you are going, you will probably end up somewhere else. You have to have goals."[31]

As humans, we are proactive creatures, not reactive. We act, which creates our surroundings, as opposed to being acted upon, becoming victims of our environment. We create our own luck and good fortune by what we choose to focus on and allow our brains to process.

In his audio presentation, *The Strangest Secret*, Earl Nightingale said these three things:

1. "You are what you think about."
2. "Every one of us is the sum total of our own thoughts."
3. "Everything you and I will ever have will come to us as the result of the way we use our minds, the one thing we possess that makes us different from all other creatures."[32]

Goals guide the mind, the mind directs our actions, and actions accomplish those goals.

The Bywater Principle

I remember when I was about ten years old, my father hired me to paint the white trim around our garage doors. I "finished" the job, and he came home from work, got out of his car, and walked straight over to the garage to inspect the work he had contracted me to do. My work thus far was subpar, splotchy painting. He directed my attention to where I had been painting, pointed to the unevenness of the paint, then looked me in the eyes and said, "If you're going to do a shoddy job, don't do it at all." He made it perfectly clear that there was no way he was going to pay me for that crude quality. My ten-year-old brain had that memory seared into it permanently. I repainted the trim, and it passed inspection the second time around. I've taken that lesson with me ever since, and as a result, I take pride in my work and don't accept sloppy, below-average results. It doesn't matter if it's painting, selling, washing dishes, or whatever—it's a waste of time and money to do a halfway job. Unfortunately, my wife and I have fired almost every housekeeper we've ever had because they all do halfway jobs and it drives us crazy! It seems to go against human nature to be thorough.

---

[31]Western, "34 Best Zig Ziglar Quotes on Leadership."
[32]Earl Nightingale, "The Strangest Secret Article," Nightingale Conant, Nightingale-Conant Corporation, http://www. nightingale.com/articles/the-strangest-secret/.

My current CEO, David Bywater, has taught that same principle repeatedly in various trainings and conference calls he's given throughout the whole country. There's a phrase he always says that resonates so well with me: "Don't play to play. Play to win." Who sets their goal to be an Olympic silver medalist? Who sets their goal to be 1st Runner-Up Miss America? Does anyone set the goal to win second at a state sport's competition? The "joy is in the journey" is nice to say . . . after you lost. While you're in the moment, you aren't thinking, "I'm just glad I'm competing." Your target, focus, dedication, and intensity are all centered around winning! If you aim for first and get third, that's okay. But if you aim for third and hit it, who cares? Who got third in the Olympics behind Michael Phelps or Usain Bolt? Ninety-nine percent of the world doesn't remember anything but the winner. If you don't aim for first, there's no chance that you'll hit it, and there's a pretty good chance you won't even place.

Just like my experience with painting, anything I do needs to be done aiming for the best result possible. Could you imagine if Best Buy was named "Second Best Buy?" Do you think Nike would sell as much if Nike was the Greek goddess of defeat rather than the personification of victory? The emotion, energy, momentum, and satisfaction that comes from winning is irreplaceable.

9 Intermission

I want you to relax and take a break from reading for a bit. I just talked about writing down goals and winning. So, I want you to ponder and think about your personal self-improvement goals and ambitions. Where do you see yourself in five years? Ten years? Decades from now? What do you want to have accomplished? I want you to skim back through the previous chapters, and write down what you've gleaned from this book thus far. Write down the impressions you had as you read my experiences and philosophies gained along the way. Is there something that you can apply in your life today? Is there a clearly defined change that you're going to make in your home life, business life, school life, or spiritual life? Do you have the desire to excel and improve and be more successful than everyone else? If that's really what you want, what are you going to do about it?

Are there business moves, education choices, or financial decisions that you would've done differently if you could go back? Life is like a "choose your own adventure" game. The choices you are consistently required to make determine your fate. I want to invite you to make a choice right now that will shape the next decade of your life. Maybe you need to adopt a healthier lifestyle. Perhaps you have to improve your work ethic. Or maybe it's time to realize that life rarely rewards those who choose the easiest path. Reading this book is a waste of your time if you don't look internally and improve your life. You aren't alone in your need to improve. You're just like me and almost 7.5 billion people who live within roughly 12,450.5 miles of you. Consider this time a gift from me to you. Breathe. Think. Internalize. Change. Love yourself; love your life. Imagine your future, write it down, and turn it into reality. You're only as good as you're willing to become. So, open your mind and set those goals.

We have some of the best content to cover coming up in the remaining chapters. I thoroughly hope you enjoy it, but more so, I hope you open your heart and your mind and realize an immediate change is possible.

"There is no avoidance in delay." — Aeschylus

What would I do if I knew I couldn't fail?

10 Balance

There are so many different activities or areas of our lives that demand our time, attention, and consistent nourishment:

THE HUMAN EXPERIENCE
- physical health and wellness
- emotional
- family
- friends
- romance
- spiritual
- personal growth and development
- work fulfillment
- environment
- fun and recreation
- financial

Likewise, the body has multiple systems that work together to make the whole body function properly.

THE HUMAN BODY
- integumentary system
- muscular system
- skeletal system
- circulatory system

- nervous system
- lymphatic system
- respiratory system
- endocrine system
- digestive system
- urinary system
- reproductive system

In both the human experience and the human body, if one area or system is neglected, then the body or life experience as a whole is affected. If one system is beaten down and fails, then there's collateral damage, and other systems take a toll and begin to fail. All areas of life are intertwined and function together; it would be difficult to succeed or even operate in one area without the support of the others. If the nervous system failed, it would affect the muscular system because the electrical impulses of the brain controls what the muscles do. In another example, the respiratory system brings oxygen into the body, and then the circulatory system carries that oxygen and other vital nutrients in the blood through the veins to the muscles and to the brain. Without that oxygen, the muscles won't function and the brain will die. That's what a stroke is: part of the brain doesn't get blood or oxygen, and it's then seriously injured or dies. Your body can only survive without oxygen for a few minutes before it goes brain dead. In fact, that's the main reason to perform CPR. Despite what Hollywood may make us believe, CPR rarely resuscitates people; its primary purpose is making sure people don't have permanent brain damage, so the aid you provide is manually performing the vital functions the lungs and heart normally perform.

If a single system stops working, is neglected or sick, it negatively impacts all the other systems either directly or indirectly. The body is like a machine that requires every piece in order to work at maximum capacity, and so it is with the human experience. For example, if I'm not doing well financially, that stress causes me to feel physically ill, consequently taking a toll on my physical health because I neglect exercise and proper nutrition. Then my marriage is strained because my wife and I argue, since I'm even less patient when I haven't exercised and have only eaten junk food. When we're upset with each other, neither of us want to clean our house, so our environment falls apart. Time for fun and leisure is non-existent because I have to work on cleaning my environment, and so on and so forth. It's a horrible domino effect that, if left unresolved, leads to a halt in progression and happiness.

The main point I'd like to make is this: treat each area of your life just like you would treat a system in your body. I don't smoke—I never have and I never will. The damage done to your respiratory system isn't worth it. Same goes for alcohol. Over time, there can be significant damage to your liver and digestive system. Is it worth it? Conversely, there are certain nutrients that are vital for each system to function correctly. I drink milk for the calcium, which fortifies my skeletal system. I eat protein-rich foods to strengthen my muscular system.

I take fish oil for the omega-3 fatty acids for the benefits to my cardiovascular system, my eyes, my brain, and probably every other system. The various areas of the human experience should be nourished just like the body. Action should be deliberately taken to strengthen and fortify those areas so they can be firing on all cylinders. If one area is neglected, then the others will unavoidably suffer as well. If you notice something is wrong with one area of your life, chances are that another area needs to be fixed.

My wife and I are huge advocates of marriage counseling. I would recommend going even when your relationship is strong and life seems smooth. Use it as a preventative measure, before you're ready to stab each other. If counseling isn't for you, here's another idea. My wife and I have noticed that in our relationship, my wife hates that I expect her to clean all the time, and I hate having a messy house. Our disorganized environment and my negative attitude was disrupting our romantic and family life. What did we do to resolve that? We hired a house-keeper; it's cheaper than marriage counseling, and you get a clean house! Or you can do both!

As discussed previously in the book when talking about your Circle of Five, having the wrong friends can negatively impact every area. Spiritual, physical, financial, emotional—you name it, and your friends and family can screw it up!

It's so important to have a regimen in place that helps you focus on each area. Habits, routines, best practices—you have to have a plan. Never stretching makes the muscular system pretty tense, so daily stretching is important to avoid injury. On the other side of things, aimlessly trying to develop spirituality is extremely ineffective; reading scriptures and some form of prayer or meditation guides you to connect to a higher power. Never reading a book makes personal growth and development a challenge, while daily listening to a book during your commute makes self-improvement nearly effortless.

In addition to a regimen, have rules, or things you will always do or never do. I will never smoke because I'm never going to jeopardize my respiratory system. Likewise, I'll never cheat on my wife because I'm never going to jeopardize my marriage. This next example may seem extreme, but I don't care, call me crazy. I made the following decision once so I didn't have to make the decision every week. For spirituality, I decided long ago that I will always go to church on a Sunday unless it was next to impossible to make it. Well, I was so committed to this decision that I jumped out of a window of a car at an intersection and walked the opposite direction to be able to attend a Sabbath service. I'm crazy committed to my rules to the point of ridicule, but that same obsession, or conviction, has helped me maintain the life-balance necessary for the $300K @ 26 way of life.

Think of some rules that you need in your life to restore or create balance. Are your friends always going out drinking, taking you away from family, work, spirituality, or exercise? Drop them. Set rules that you will never break. Have your own moral code that you live by and never compromise. What are some habits that need to change or a regimen or rules that needs to be put in place? Write them down. You're already thinking about it right now, so write it down and then execute it.

Jack of All Trades, Master of None, versus the Specialist

The phrase "Jack of All Trades" was originally a very positive statement referring to an individual who could do everything. "Master of None" was later added to this figure of speech, and the connotation suddenly changed from positive to negative. Adding that phrase is almost like adding a disclaimer; it implies that an individual's knowledge of each field is superficial and not as valuable as it could otherwise be. So, then the question arises: should I be a Jack of all trades or not? To answer this question, I'm going to illustrate this point with two examples:

The Handyman. What can a handyman do? Everything, right? They can unclog toilets, paint, replace siding, mow lawns, do basic electrical work, roofing, tree trimming, tile work, fix just about anything, change oil in a car, carpentry, etc. That list goes on and on! What does a handyman get paid for his work? Peanuts. Get a bid for painting a room from a painting company versus a handyman, and I guarantee there will be a tremendous difference in price. I also guarantee there will be a difference in quality and time that it takes to finish the job.

The Family Doctor. My dad is a family doctor/general practitioner. He is the "handyman" of medicine. Growing up, he always told me that when he was in school, the medical students who got poor grades went on to become specialists because they didn't have to remember as much. To be a family doctor, you had to remember almost everything you learned in school because you would be using it throughout your entire career. What does a family doctor make versus a surgeon? Peanuts. What does a general surgeon make versus a plastic surgeon or a neurosurgeon? Peanuts. Specialists make a ridiculously higher amount of money than those who have no specialty. You pay more because they went to school for a few more years and learned significantly more about just one body part or mastered one difficult skill. The cost may also be higher because there's less demand for their services, the more specialized they become. They could be ultra-specialized in a disease or medical technique that is extremely rare. Because there are barriers to entry in their field, they get more business and justify the higher prices because their services are more exclusive and there's an inelastic demand for them specifically.

On the flipside, there can be serious consequences to overspecialization. If a doctor spends all their time learning their trade and doesn't learn at least a little bit about other topics that are relevant to success, there will potentially be some costly shortcomings. As an example, doctors are notorious for mismanagement of personal finances. I wonder why that could be? Could it be that the rigorous coursework, endless studying, and insane hours of hospital rotations stunted their growth in other vital areas of understanding? Knowledge about money and learning financial discipline is so important to overall health, stability, and well-being. What else is jeopardized for the sake of specialization? Are social skills underdeveloped? What about family relationships? Business management? If they're so laser focused on just one thing, it can be easy to forget about the big picture. They're going to need to do more than just get a degree. They have to build a business after medical school.

So, how do you find balance between these two ideas? Should an individual be a "Jack of All Trades" or a specialist in their life and profession? The next chapter touches on the idea of staying put so you can spend the 10,000 hours required to master a field. I absolutely believe it's important to master one skill or talent and learn how to do it better than everyone else. This mastery, however, shouldn't be done at the expense of gaining an understanding of how the world operates. If you don't know how to make a budget, but you can make a ton of money, you'll probably be just as stressed as someone making a tenth of your income and living paycheck to paycheck.

In my career, I've noticed that as I learn more about the various operations of our business, I'm better able to explain the big picture. As counterintuitive as this sounds, the deeper my understanding of my product and business, the easier it is for me to simplify and sell to my customers. Not just that, but as a salesman, if I don't understand at least the basics of what other people do for work or as a hobby, it's harder to connect with them on a personal level and have a meaningful conversation.

As a teenager, I started to learn how to find a balance between specialization and learning bits of various skills. High school was the best of times for some and the worst of times for most. Just about everyone fit into a clique or classification and did everything exclusively with that group of people. There are a few people who are accepted into a range of groups; they are what I call "social chameleons." These rare individuals were essentially diplomats who crossed clique lines on a daily basis and brought cohesion to the teenager ecosystem. After we were married, my wife and I realized that we were both chameleons. We could fit in with a wider range of personalities than most people could. We were people pleasers. I don't think I was popular, but I definitely socialized with a wider variety of people than most students did. It didn't matter who you were, I would talk to you and be your friend.

With that, I had a reasonable amount of talent in music, art, and drama, but I excelled at sports and academics. I knew a little bit about each clique, but I had my main focus on sports and academics because I knew that's where I was most likely to get money for a scholarship. When I found out I wasn't a good enough swimmer to get a scholarship, I invested all my extra time in reaching the top of the academic totem pole. As a result of that effort, I earned a scholarship worth $80K. In the end, I chose to use the academic path to reach my income goal and I mastered that field.

Knowing a lot can enhance and magnify the power of specialization. I've seen these principles of specializing and having a wide variety of interests and knowledge with my career today. I know a little bit about a lot of different topics; I've developed talents in many areas and have various hobbies that I do well enough. However, with that diversity of knowledge and talent, I know a *ton* about selling and even more about my product specifically. That diversity of knowledge has taught me how to cater to most personalities, and as a result, I've seen huge success. Knowing a little bit about a lot of things has amplified my specialization in sales. I'm all right at playing basketball and racquetball. People who don't play piano think I'm amazing, but compared to people who actually play piano, I'm mediocre. I'm pretty average to above average in lots of areas of my life, but then, I'm a sales specialist.

Not only does knowing a lot magnify that specialization, but it also makes life interesting and worth living. There's a saying I learned my first day in Spanish class, "*En la variedad está el gusto*," which in English is equivalent to, "Variety is the spice of life." Why master a field if you sacrifice culture and enjoyment? If the other aspects of your life are failing miserably, it isn't worth specializing. If your success is at the cost of sacrificing a pure, unadulterated, and happy life, is it really success? I've heard so many times to pick a career that you love. Then the supposed secret to real success is to bury yourself in that beloved career. I love my wife's homemade fried chicken. If that's all I ever ate, I would probably hate it *and* I would probably die pretty young. (In my life insurance application, I think there might've been a section where they ask about risky activities, like skydiving and frequency of eating fried chicken.)

Variety *is* the spice of life. So, go out there and develop various talents, pursue multiple interests, and have more than just a fulfilling career. Sure, you can love your job, but do other things with your life.

Man, I'm really craving some fried chicken now . . .

Political Neutrality

Learning how to talk or not talk about politics goes right along with the idea of becoming a chameleon. It's incredibly important to be agreeable. Sales success and success in most areas of life typically involve making friends. In Jeffrey Gitomer's *The Little Red Book of Selling*, he lists "12.5 Reasons Why People Buy." The number-one reason listed is, "I like my sales rep." Politics is such an easy topic to stir up disagreements and discord; it's one of the easiest ways to get someone to *not* like you. The United States is almost evenly divided between two major parties, which have platforms that don't quite agree with one another. I personally have pretty strong political opinions rooted in my understanding of economics and history, but my stances aren't aligned fully with either major political party. I made the mistake of engaging in political hostility with a family member about five years ago. That individual leans very strongly toward one of the major parties—there's still tension there that will likely never go away. Learn from your mistakes, right? Since then, I've adopted an attitude of political neutrality. I read the platform for both of the major parties and had the realization that both sides are human. Both parties have good and bad points; neither is perfect. So, how can you use this to your advantage?

A good number of the conversations I had with my customers this past year involved anywhere from a brief to a lengthy chat about the 2016 presidential election, especially as we got closer to that great and dreadful Election Day. I agreed with the positive and I agreed with the negative. It's interesting: when you stop and listen to what people are saying, more often than not, they're fighting for something that both sides can and should agree on. There are exceptions, of course, but in sales, you need to avoid arguments at all costs!

The easiest question I ask people is, "What do/did you think of the election?" or "What do you think of this candidate?" Whatever they say, I listen intently and nod my head, validating their points. Usually what they say is humorous and pretty spot on, so we share a laugh. Even if I personally prefer the other candidate, it doesn't matter because my goal is to find common ground and embrace that common ground.

The bottom line here is respect. It doesn't matter if it's politics, religion, gender identity, sexual orientation, views on immigration, or whatever! I'm not here to judge your thoughts or feelings. I'm here to thoughtfully listen, seek to truly understand your perspective, and then be agreeable. I will gladly sell you my product no matter who you are . . . unless you don't pay your bills and have bad credit, then I will never sell you anything unless you get your act together. Black, white, green, blue, gay, straight, ugly, beautiful, tall, short, smart, dumb—whoever you are, we have to have at least *something* in common, and I'm going to try to find it and not dwell on our differences.

The validation that people receive when you take time to listen to them and seek to understand goes a long way. Most people have a strong opinion about politics, so that's why I bring it up. It gives them the chance to be *heard* in a setting where they won't be told they're wrong or a racist, a sexist, a socialist, or an idiot. By doing this, even if I don't fully agree, I'm on their side because they realize that I respect them and care about their thoughts and feelings. That reassurance then gives me the chance to share my thoughts and feelings about my product openly, allowing a sale to take place.

11 10,000 Hours—Don't Contract "The Grass Is Greener" Syndrome

Exponential Growth Takes Time

Malcolm Gladwell popularized the idea that it takes 10,000 hours of practice or experience in order to achieve "mastery" in a field.

My two-year LDS mission was a defining time in my life. Not only did I meet my wife, but I met my current career and calling in door-to-door sales. Throughout that time, I learned the mentality and discipline of daily study, planning, hard work, knocking on strangers' doors, facing tons of rejection, getting referrals, teaching people to understand new concepts, transferring enthusiasm for something I'm passionate about, tracking numbers based on key indicators, training new "recruits," and training a team. Some of those days included studying up to eight hours and riding a bicycle in triple-digit temperatures with 100-percent humidity wearing a suit and tie. The only "time off" I had for two years was sleep at night, which was exactly eight hours every night, and on Mondays, I got about six hours of time to go shopping, write letters, and maybe play a little basketball. That comes out to 106 hours each week. Let's round that number down to 100, so for two full years, we'll call 100 weeks. That comes out to exactly 10,000 hours learning the skills necessary to be successful with my current job. Why would I have done anything else other than a profession that uses all those skills? I had 10,000 hours under my belt before I even made a dime; why not utilize that skillset to make money? Take out the bike, suit, and tie, and the description of those two years almost perfectly matches what my daily work routine looks like today.

My original plan was to come home from my mission, finish my undergrad degree, and then go to medical school. I would've started on an arduous path where I would've had to spend 10,000 hours mastering basic medicine in medical school, then taken 10,000 hours in residency to master my actual specialty. Finally after finishing all that school, I would have to take another 10,000 hours to master running a business, which would include hiring employees, firing employees, finances, and time management. It's amazing that anyone can run a successful medical practice after jumping through so many hoops to get licensed just to be able to start their business. I would've been exhausted and ready to retire after working for maybe ten years tops. I consciously chose not to take that path because I wanted to utilize my energy already spent mastering one extremely useful skillset and then use my remaining energy to capitalize on that two-year experience.

The compound effect mentioned earlier, the 10,000-hour rule, and the hedgehog concept work hand in hand. I first learned about the hedgehog concept from the book, *Good to Great*. It asserts that organizations or individuals have a much higher probability of success if they focus on one thing and do it as well as they possibly can. I chose to be a hedgehog and just use the only skill I had really ever known.

Few people will ever serve an LDS mission and experience that rigor and discipline. There are currently around 40,000 new missionaries every year, and there are about 131,000,000 people born in the world each year. To serve an LDS mission makes you one in 3,275. A mission isn't going to be the experience that everyone takes to achieve massive success. This is the path that I chose for myself, and I credit a huge amount of my success to this experience because it was a rigorous, extremely structured program that demanded a lot out of me. There are so many other avenues to achieve similar self-discipline and work ethic and 10,000 hours learning a valuable skillset. Some examples would be:

- serving in any branch of the military, the Navy SEALs especially
- attending an Ivy League university and fulfilling the requirements to receive a degree
- training and competing in elite high school, college, and professional sports programs
- training to be a special agent at the FBI Academy in Quantico, Virginia
- GE's Green Beret program to train top-level executives

There are tons of other examples. My mission for me was like my own premier training academy, where I spent thousands of hours learning and developing a skillset that would one day bring me to my current position. I spent two years *completely* dedicated to my missionary responsibilities and tasks—as I said before, there were strict rules like no movies, no dating, and no video games. Furthermore, I was only allowed thirty minutes of morning exercise, I had mandatory three to four hours of daily study and new missionary training, and then we filled the rest of the day with seemingly endless hours of service projects, planning, prospecting, and teaching religious lessons. This was basically all day, every day, for 104 weeks. I left my mission feeling like anything else I did afterward would be a total piece of cake in comparison. However, instead of leaving behind all that specialized knowledge and experience, I chose to do a job that is extremely similar in nature to my two years of service. I took all the wisdom from that religious experience and applied it to the business world. What a difference it made!

The following graph illustrates the progression of my income, including those two years of unpaid service/training.

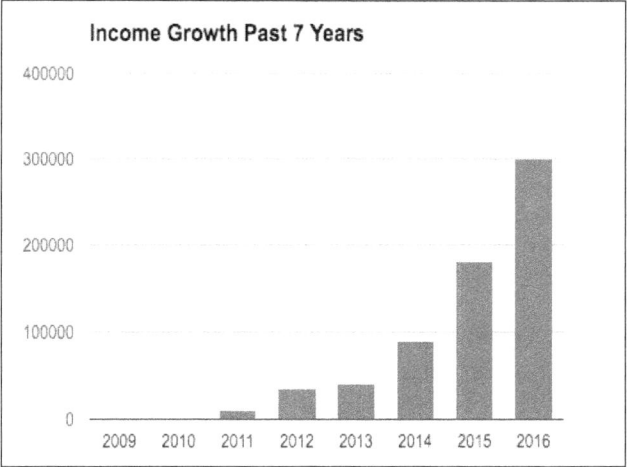

Image 13

Exponential growth is a beautiful thing. The point where exponential growth takes place is after you reach 10,000 hours of practice. The compounding occurs after becoming a hedgehog, sticking to the same thing, mastering it, and then suddenly slipping into a surreal flow of success.

As I've been learning and developing, I've noticed an interesting trend. The longer I stay put, working in the same neighborhood, town, or even the same state, the more success I achieve. I have had to consciously force myself to keep working in the same area. During my first year of summer sales, I used to get dropped off in a neighborhood, go door-to-door, knock on every house, and be totally done with an entire neighborhood in one or two days. In my mind, there were no more sales to be had by anyone because I had already knocked on every door. The first time I made it a full week without moving to a new neighborhood, I was blown away by the difference in the level of success I experienced. In 2013, not only was I constantly changing neighborhoods to work in, but we were also constantly moving from hotel to hotel; in the span of ten weeks, we had moved ten times! The level of improvement that I experienced from 2012 to 2013 seemed insignificant because of this instability and lack of a chance to build momentum. In 2016, I bought a house, essentially forcing myself to stay put. It made such a difference in my success; since I'd already reached 10,000 hours selling for my company, my next step was to reach 10,000 hours selling my product to the same demographic and culture in my little town. The longer I'm there, the better I'll get. I have seen and will see more exponential growth the longer I spend working in my town. The next section explains a big reason this principle is true.

Longevity = Credibility, Trust, and Repeat Business

There are a handful of questions that I get very regularly from just about all my prospective customers. "How long have you been with the company?" actually means, "Once I sign up, how long will you stick around?" When I get that question, I'm able to respond with, "About five or six years." I remember the expressions people would make years ago when I was responding, "Five or six weeks . . ." There was a certain level of discomfort and uneasiness from them, and my voice consequently went up about an octave because my confidence was drowning. Every customer knew there was a good chance that they would never see me again, and while they liked me, they needed to trust that when I was long gone, I was leaving them in capable hands.

To overcome that doubt, I had to have an air of confidence that made me appear as if I'd been working there for decades. It was super tough back then to get started. I had to "sell" the company way more than I do now. I had to talk about reviews and customer service, etc. Now, I *am* the company, I *am* the customer service—I'm a living breathing review because I actually know what's going on. At this point, I mainly only need to sell myself; once my customers know I'm competent and trustworthy, they'll believe my company can be trusted too. When comparing myself to the competition who had just started, it's easier to believe that I'm the one who's most likely to be there to help twenty years later when they need to put new solar panels on their roof. It's easier to believe that if they have an issue, they can text me and I'll do my best to take care of them. It goes from being a simple transactional relationship, like a fast-food purchase, to a long-term relationship of trust and fidelity.

Ten thousand hours goes a lot further if it's in the same industry, at the same company, in the same state. Jumping around destroys your credibility, not only with your customers but also with your employees. Who wants to jump around from career to career, company to company, or state to state? I've done the state-to-state thing, and let me tell you, it's miserable! Not worth it. People generally know that jumping around isn't the answer, and they don't want to follow someone who can't anchor down and establish a grounded, successful life. Now, this only applies under the circumstances of working for the right company, at the right place, at the right time. If those conditions aren't met, then you may have to jump around a bit till you get it right. Don't perpetually look for something better, though; water the grass where you're planted, and it will grow greener and healthier the longer you're there caring for it. I made the most money I've ever made in a year because I mostly stayed put. That was despite a move to the next town over, buying our first home, and the smooth yet stressful birth of our third daughter. I settled down, committed, and was ready to build a dynasty right there.

Opportunities may one day arise for me to be able to expand and grow, which may necessitate moving. However, when making a move or a change, it's important to look five to ten years into the future and ask yourself if Future You will thank Current You for making that change. Is a loss of momentum worth a title/promotion? When you move, it's like the transition from being a high school senior to a freshman in college. In high school, you work your way up to be the top dog. Everyone knows you; you're basically a celebrity. Then you move to the next arena, where suddenly you're at the bottom of the totem pole and have to start all over again. Whether it's your customers or employees, you have to re-establish trust and credibility, which takes time.

The fruits of that longevity and permanence are wonderful. There's something beautiful that comes from customers that feels like a gift from heaven. It's called repeat business. The joys of repeat business have to be experienced to get the full effect; simply attempting to describe it wouldn't do that exquisite euphoria a joule of justice. Repeat business only comes over time after you've made a significant investment in your customers. It only comes if you've delighted your customers and went above and beyond to help them. I've personally made hundreds of thousands of dollars from repeat and referral business already. It's so much easier for people to buy from you a second time and refer others because they've already been through the process; their concerns were already resolved once, and they know the experience that their friends can expect. As a result, they don't ask questions the second time around, so the sale portion of the interaction is almost nonexistent. You did the work the first time, and it pays dividends the longer you spend in the same place with the same company working with the same customer base. You're just expected to handle everything for your customers, and they *trust* you. They trust that just like the first and second and third time around, you'll take care of them.

A common retirement plan is to save up millions of dollars and then live off of the interest that that money generates. If you have $1.5 million saved up, you will gain an additional $105,000 every year just by earning a 7 percent return on that nest egg. So, without eating into that principal, you can make a six-figure income. Treat your customer base like you're saving up $1.5 million. As long as you have a good product, your customers will absolutely yield a return/dividend, whether it's coming from referrals or from repeat business. Building up that lucrative client portfolio takes a great deal of time. The beauty of staying put is that there comes a tipping point where once you have so many customers, the majority of your new business will come from repeat business. This $300K year was a result of passing that tipping point.

When I first moved to Connecticut about two years ago, my job description was totally different. It started out as a grind, where I would go door-to-door for eight-plus hours a day, six days a week. Less than 10 percent of people I talked to moved forward with buying my product. They weren't referrals, it wasn't repeat business, they were cold calls—not cold like ice cream cold, it was cold like a windstorm in the middle of February in North Dakota and no one wants to do anything because it's so miserably cold, cold. My tipping point came once I had a solid core of customers who were basically ready to start selling for me. They warmed up the entire town, and even the towns around them by talking about my product to their friends, family members, neighbors, coworkers—they've even talked to strangers on the train to NYC! As it stands today (depending on the week, but in general), it's probably between 25–50 percent of the people I talk to become customers. If I'm self-generating business, then it's on the lower end. If my customers are generating my business for me, then it's probably around 75 percent or more that go forward. What this means is through referrals, I need two to four conversations in order to gain a customer. When I first started, that ratio was approximately ten to twenty conversations needed to gain a customer. Later in the book, I'll touch on this conversion ratio more when I talk about working smarter, not harder.

The fruits of longevity, of 10,000 hours working with your customer base, are only reaped by those who are patient and persistent. If you're impatient and always jumping around, you'll never get to see your job description change from a grind to the retirement plan just collecting interest. I earned over 66 percent more in 2016 than I did 2015. However, I was way more stressed out and worked way harder in 2015.

My life has been full of too much moving; for the past ten years, I've jumped around for work, church, and school to these places:

- Winter Haven
- Eagle Lake
- Lander
- Laramie
- Provo
- Jupiter
- Orlando
- Kissimmee
- Lake Buenaventura
- Oviedo
- Lander

- Sacramento
- Laramie
- Little Rock
- Jonesboro
- Fort Smith
- Laramie
- Amarillo
- San Antonio
- Cheyenne
- Uvalde
- Beaumont
- Lafayette
- Baton Rouge
- Laramie
- Colby
- Laramie
- Lake Charles
- Stockton
- Phoenix
- Peoria
- Hamden
- North Haven

As I've moved less, I've been more successful. The last few times I've jumped around have been with my current company. The moving gradually slowed down, and there was a direct correlation between that stability and my income. In 2014, I started working in Stockton, California, where I only worked for a month. Within that office in Stockton, I moved my work area three or four times. I then moved to the deserts of Arizona, where for some reason, I thought the grass would be greener. I stayed there for about eight months, and again, I switched my work areas in Phoenix about three times. And finally, I moved to Connecticut, where I've been in the same area for about two years. I anchored down and decided to water and fertilize the grass where I landed. As a result, my income in 2016 was about the same as the three previous years combined!

The grass is green where you make it green, but it takes ridiculously hard work and an insane degree of patience. I've wanted to rip all my hair out a few times. My hair has gone a little gray in spots—not too bad, though. I'm also not ashamed to admit that I've cried numerous times. But . . . oh, how wonderful it is to see the fruits of your labor after planting, watering, and fertilizing. It's a wonderful feeling when a $6,000 weekly check is the norm. There's a new quality of life and freedom that can't be replaced. I can promise you that you won't regret making a lot of money; it's worth the stress, it's worth the pain and grief. It's essential to remember that the law of the harvest is only fulfilled when you plant, nurture, and then wait as your fruits grow and multiply. If I had stayed in Stockton, the title of this book would've included a dollar amount higher than $300K . . . as long as I didn't get shot in a drive-by. Stay put as long as you can! Although, as I said, it is important that you don't necessarily sacrifice every single new challenge and growth opportunity that comes your way. Eventually moving might make sense. Try to get the moving and jumping around out of your system early on, and then commit to a location and claim it. Own it. Dominate it.

Grow Organically; Don't Sacrifice Loyalty for a Title

Throughout life, people may attempt to flatter you in order to "poach you." They'll tell you that you deserve better; they'll describe your current company like it's an abusive spouse. Of course they're going to say that! Of course your competition wants you to leave and work for them instead! You're worth more to them because not only are you bringing them added value, you're also hurting the enemy. With these offers comes fancy new made-up titles. How special is the title of VP if everyone is a VP? How about the title of manager if they're giving everything with a heartbeat that title? It's so easy to skip a step in your progression. It's easy to jump from a mediocre performance to a fancy title when someone offers it to you. What's there to lose? It was easy, more money, and a shiny title for less work. That's the dream, right? Unfortunately, you sacrifice some very crucial educational experiences by taking that route.

Why weren't you promoted with your first company? What were you missing? When you skip a step, you've suddenly developed a dependency. Could you go and create your own company from scratch? Chances are that you didn't learn something vital in the process. Like a parent who buys their kids whatever they want and teaches their children to be dependent rather than independent, you've been given something for nothing. What happens when that company goes bankrupt and you have to start all over? Could you start your own company and get to the same point on your own? Probably not, you missed something. Will the company you abandoned for that shiny new title want you back? I doubt it. Maybe begrudgingly. Although, we had someone named Lance leave recently to a competitor, and I don't believe I could ever think anything negative toward him. If he ever came back, like in the Parable of the Prodigal Son, I would slaughter the fatted calf, throw him a party, and put a ring on his finger. However, that individual's outstanding character makes him an exception; in most cases, you're a traitor and a fair-weather friend. You weren't equally invested in the success of your friends' and coworkers' business. On top of that, I've seen the weight of guilt damn progression and a return to normalcy. How to avoid that: loyalty. Make the choice to commit to your team once, so you don't have to decide every single week if times are tough if you're going to stick around or not.

So, when people abandon ship, what could that missing ingredient be that they skipped and didn't learn because they left? Maybe it was humility. Maybe you didn't get the position and title you wanted because you needed to humble yourself so people would actually like you and want to work with you long term.

Maybe you were lacking persistence. What if you gave up right before you were going to get the same promotion with your first company? If someone says they're leaving for another company to get their title, do you think anyone would see them the same? Why would anyone offer them any kind of promotion if they're ready to walk away? That's not the kind of person you want on the boat. So, don't be that person!

Maybe the missing element was passion. Maybe you needed to buy in to your product, company, or cause just a little more, and that would've been the difference. An extra ounce of passion compounded daily makes a huge difference. Passion is perhaps one of the key differences between the average and the exceptional.

I want to be clear that there is a time and a place for leaving your company. When you're undervalued, under-appreciated, and truly unhappy, you need to make a change. It does have to be the right company, at the right place, at the right time. It's possible that there really is some major unresolvable issue that makes the deck stacked eternally against you. In many cases, though, the grass is not greener somewhere else. Titles and promotions can often be earned where you're planted, but only through hard work, persistence, dedication, and loyalty. These attributes represent some of the core fundamentals of business; without a firm grasp on these principles, advancing will always evade you.

I first gained an understanding of this principle of learning the fundamentals in math class years ago; it was in my Quantum Mechanics course in college. I remember doing one single math problem that would take multiple hours and multiple sheets of paper to solve. I always wondered why we had to do any of the calculations out by hand if we could simply plug the equation and variables into a calculator and get the answer instantly. We had to learn the basics, gradually adding little twists and turns, until eventually, we were working on some of the most complex problems anyone had ever solved. We were establishing a foundational knowledge that would support and provide clarity to the more difficult theorems and principles. This fundamental knowledge is what guided people much smarter than me to write the computer programs that now solve those ultra-complex problems in an instant.

I remember my professor saying, what if all computers disappeared, or what if the batteries in your calculator die and your airplane crashed on a desert island and you need to rebuild a new airplane by scratch? The odds are slim that that will happen; however, the fundamental knowledge is what has led to many technological innovations. Someone was sick of wasting tons of paper and time solving these complex math problems so they innovated and found a solution worth billions of dollars.

There's a reason that certain classes have prerequisite courses. It's because without understanding the previous courses' principles, you'll probably flunk. I took Calculus 1 and Calculus 2 before I took a hiatus from school and served a mission for two years. I didn't think about Calculus once during that time, and I gradually forgot just about everything I had learned. I came back home from my mission and decided I should take Calculus 3, which had Calculus 1 and 2 listed as prerequisites. This was because it combined the principles of the two courses and then added another dimension or two. It was a horrible class for me. I got my first "B" since the sixth grade. The following semester, I took Quantum Mechanics, which had Calculus 3 as a prerequisite, and so as a result, it only got worse from there. I already had a weak foundation and shaky understanding, which only degraded further the more advanced the subject matter became. It felt like I was building a Jenga tower higher and higher each time I advanced to the next course; I was ready to topple. That class yielded my only "C" ever (excluding my "S" grade in fourth grade, which may have actually been the same as an "F" note). I don't even know if I deserved a grade that generous.

Leadership and personal development are no different. There's a natural order to growth: skip a step, and you'll either really struggle or fail completely. Those fundamentals come little by little. Working to earn your stripes will lead to extreme success and ultimately, a sense of ownership, satisfaction, and pride for what you've accomplished.

In sales, I've seen so many high-earning people "burn out." These individuals seem to be the one-hit wonders of the industry; they get started with so much fire and drive, performing for a couple quarters or even a couple years, and then suddenly, they fizzle out. I've witnessed a common trend with those people who are struggling after a brief stint of success. They start to spend money like an NBA player, but then they stop training like a professional athlete. Consequently, there's a huge drop in income. They then become desperate for money, and their judgment turns cloudy. They begin to feel like they're never going to get promoted or make enough money to keep their baller lifestyle. They finally give in to the temptation to go somewhere else where they know they'll be promoted immediately and be treated like a king again—at least for a short period of time.

We recently had someone leave to a rival competitor that isn't even in the same league as our company. One of my coworkers, Nicholas Howard, gave this beautiful sports analogy to describe the situation: "Some people want to go play for the Cleveland Browns to be a standout. Others want to play for the Patriots and be part of a winning culture and succeed with the best of them." That was totally spot on! Who's going to have more drive and incentive to improve and learn and grow: a big fish in a little pond or a little fish in a big pond?

Now this isn't me discouraging entrepreneurship; on the contrary, I highly recommend starting and leading your own business. What I'm referring to is stepping down a league or two to get recognized rather than growing organically by working harder, getting gritty, becoming hyper-focused, upping the intensity, grabbing the bull by the horns, and claiming your desired position or level of success. If you try to skip your 10,000 hours, then that success has a high probability of being short lived. Jumping around won't fix a major underlying issue like work ethic, for example. The 10,000-hour rule is synonymous with the phrase, "Paying your dues." Patience is more than just a virtue; it's a key that unlocks higher levels of achievement, career advancement, and lasting wealth.

Chapter 11: 10,000 Hours—Don't Contract "The Grass Is Greener" Syndrome

12 Confidence

Swagger

I recently had one of my electricians call me while on site, ready to begin a solar installation. He said that my customer wanted to remove more than half of the panels from his design because he supposedly "didn't agree to the design." Not true. I told my electrician to put me on the phone with the customer. "I one-hundred-percent promise you'll love it. It's going to look like you have a brand-new roof. Most people just don't want them on the front, yours are all on the back, it'll be fine . . ." The tone of my voice was, "Man, you and I both know this whole thing is going on your roof." This was after two to three hours of my installers trying to figure out what's going on. I got on the phone for a minute, and the deal was finally closed. Assume it, baby! His response was, "Just have my wife sign off on it, I don't want to." Done deal!

The end to that story is that I greatly over-delivered to those homeowners. My company threw out an awesome incentive to try to help us push more customers forward to getting solar panels installed. I didn't mention this to her, but she was put on the list to receive $1,000, and I think the email letting her know went to her junk mail. She called me a few days after her install in disbelief, wondering if the check my company sent her was legitimate. I told her, "Merry Christmas! I promise the check won't bounce."

After both of these phone calls, my posture somehow was perfect. My chest was flexed like a cocky rooster. I did a chin pop and an air kiss to my four-year-old and said "Wassup?!" I felt like beating on my chest like King Kong. I think I might have after that first call—I felt like I had just dominated life and I could take on anything.

In *Be Obsessed or Be Average*, Grant Cardone talks about the notion of over-promising and then over-delivering—not under-promising and over-delivering. He says that you don't want to start your relationship with your customer like a wimp. Don't be a scared baby. Promise people the world, and then give them the world and $1,000!

Meeting Expectations

Expectations is a little-known secret that is necessary to succeed. Having high expectations from my trainees, peers, and superiors drastically improves my performance. In our office, we have competitions all the time; we recently ran one where we did a draft-style pick for mini-sales teams within our office that would compete with each other for a week. I got the first pick. I picked a rep who was shocked that I picked him first. He didn't think he deserved to be first pick. His performance was incredible that week! He probably had his most successful week ever. He texted me and told me that he didn't want to let me down; he felt this push because he was picked first. He knew I was confident in his abilities, and he wanted to rise up to meet those expectations.

I have two main sources of income from my current position. I personally go out and knock on doors, selling my product, and I manage a team that goes out and sells my product as well. I get an override, or a cut, of the commission from everything my reps sell. This is because I'm responsible for recruiting, training, leading and motivating them. This past year, I made less than 10 percent of my income from those overrides. More than 90 percent of the money I made came from my personal sales production. Looking at the time I spend with managing, close to half of the time I spend at my job is what's making me 10 percent of my money. Why not just step down as a manager and take that time and dedicate it to my personal sales? I would probably make more money, right? Wrong. First of all, I find fulfillment in helping others to succeed. Second of all, I have way higher expectations from upper management and my *entire team* to perform at a level that is double what my typical rep does. I'm held to a higher standard because of my position. If I were to leave that role, I would walk away from the confidence and expectations of everyone. From my experience, it seems like it's human nature to do what people expect you to. There's an intangible energy that comes from the people who are watching; when they want and expect your success, it's way more likely to happen. The best analogy I can think of is comparing this to a home court advantage.

I read a fascinating article titled, "Home Advantage in Sports: A Scientific Study of How Much It Affects Winning." It talks about how there would be a noticeable difference if professional sports teams were allowed to play all of their games at home versus having to travel. Here's an excerpt from that article:

> We know that home-field, -court, and -ice advantage is real. Teams win more games at home. I wondered, though, whether we over-value or under-value such an advantage, so I nerded out and crunched some numbers.

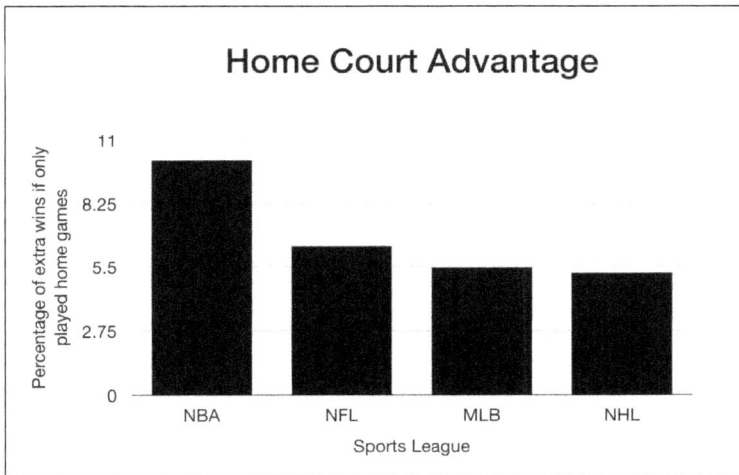

Home Court Advantage

Image 14: Home Court Advantage

In other words, to take an example: based on the number of games an average NBA team won at home over the past three years, it projects to have won 10.11% more game if it were allowed to play all its contests at home. To extend this example: this advantage would transform a 41-win team into a 45-win team. That isn't an enormous improvement, but it might just be enough to shove a team into the playoffs.[33]

There are many factors that could contribute to this advantage. A big reason comes from the psychological aspect; the home team's fans don't have to travel as far to attend the game, and consequently, the home team will almost always have significantly more support from the crowd. When the crowd is cheering you on, it boosts your ego, giving you a shot of endorphins and a newfound energy.

---

[33] Jon Bois, "Home Advantage in Sports: A Scientific Study of How Much It Affects Winning," SBNATION, Vox Media, infographic, accessed 17 October 2017, https://www.sbnation.com/2011/1/19/1940438/home-field-advantage-sports-stats-data.

You suddenly feel a sense of responsibility, almost an obligation, to perform for your fans. It's easier to dunk when you're trying to impress the people wearing jerseys with *your* name on it.

The bottom line is, put yourself in a position that demands results. Having accountability to your superiors, peers, and trainees will boost your performance, ultimately pushing you to the next level of success.

So, did I only make 10 percent or so of my income from my position? Nope! The impact of my peers' demand for my success and their confidence in my potential was immeasurable. The spotlight is where we perform best. Get there ASAP and let psychology handle the rest.

Training Does More for Me Than for the Trainee

For more than two years, I've been the go-to person in our office for new reps to shadow when they start working with our company. They follow me around for a day or two so they can learn the ropes and see how the whole process works. For some reason, my performance is typically two to three times better when I have someone with me. It's the same effect that I would imagine performance-enhancing drugs like steroids or Adderall would have. With that shadow, I seem to say all the right things, any stuttering or stammering goes away, and I turn into the smoothest version of myself. It's because I'm being watched and I feel the pressing need to succeed. A little over a year ago, I had one of the worst experiences of my career while I had a brand-new rep shadowing me. My wife was mad at me, and in the middle of that, I had an awful experience with a customer and a competitor while my trainee was with me. I was so angry! I wanted to call it quits and go home for the rest of the year and live off of ice cream and Netflix, wallowing in my pain. Well, you can't do that when someone brand new is watching you, learning from you and taking notes on everything you do and say. So, I used that anger as fuel to perform better. Within the space of a few hours, I created as much new business for our company as most reps create in a whole week. Those new clients from that day have since compounded into three times as much business. And to top it off, that brand-new rep is now managing a team by my side, and he has become one of the best recruiters I've ever met!

The teacher often reaps more than the student because the principles and lessons taught are reinforced to the teacher. Leadership gives a striking new confidence; it forces you to grow into whatever capacity you need to. If we are properly cared for by the people around us and are surrounded by fans cheering for us or trainees depending on us, then likewise, we will never stop growing either.

13 The Marriage Advantage

This was the toughest chapter to write, hands down. I would be remiss to not include at least a short chapter about the truly marvelous impact this magnificent woman has had on my life. We're going on eight years since we met, and those eight years have flown by (minus my time doing summer sales—that felt like an eternity)! I think the value of a help meet that ameliorates your character and soul on a daily basis is worth more than what any amount of money or power can buy or do. Regardless of your beliefs, this idea stems back at least thousands of years, and it is the foundation upon which society is built: *"And the Lord God said, 'It is not good that the man should be alone; I will make him an help meet for him.'"*[34] I believe that it is not good for me to be alone because I'm my best self with my soulmate. If someone ever mentions something good about me or pays me a compliment, I believe my wife and I are so unified that she deserves just as much credit for my success. I'll just share a couple ideas that I have about marriage. (It won't include a discussion on the tax implications of getting married, but you should definitely look into those benefits!)

---

[34]Gen. 2:18

1+1=3

As I reflect on the years I've spent with my wife, I'm amazed at how that time has created an increase in accountability, purpose, drive, support, friendship, delicious food, stability, access to more ideas, memory, knowledge, and an instant doubling of wisdom from our combined decades of experience. Our steady commitment to one another has enriched each one of those aspects of our lives, allowing us to succeed in and out of the home.

The idea of a spouse improving memory is intriguing. As bad as this may sound, my millennial brain instantly thinks of electronics when I hear the word "memory." With that twenty-first century definition of memory, what's the difference between thirty-two gigs and sixty-four gigs of memory on your smartphone? Have you ever had to go back through your photos and videos and decide which ones to delete to make room to download a new app? It makes my blood boil when my phone says I have to go through and free up memory. The worst is when you have so little memory that it won't even download your new emails. This isn't something that happens in nature; when you go on a family vacation and you're making some of the best memories of your life, your brain doesn't just suddenly stop and say, "Before you can do anything else, you need to delete old memories." With electronics, though, you're constantly having to free up space or increase memory. In electronics, the difference when you double memory is huge! It gives you capacity to record and preserve twice as many songs, twice as many pictures, twice as many videos, twice as many apps, twice as many emails and texts, twice as many games—you name it, it's doubled.

There's a difference with marriage; it isn't like taking two hard drives and putting them together. There's an intangible synergy that comes from matrimony that makes each individual more than what they were before they said, "I do." Marriage has more than doubled my memory. Somehow, the laws of math and computer science are transcended by this infinitely rewarding relationship; somehow, 1+1=3. It defies logic, but reality doesn't always follow the theorems and laws invented by mathematicians. My wife and I both have bits and pieces of the whole picture. When we communicate with each other and discuss our memories, it makes it so each of us remembers more details that would've otherwise been stuck in our subconscious. We talk and counsel with one another, and new ideas and new memories are created. Artificial intelligence doesn't come close to replicating what two humans with similar goals and synergy can create. Marriage has doubled many things in my life, but it has tripled my potential.

My wife and I wrote letters for two years before we even went on a date. During those two years, our relationship was formed around a foundation of lifting and encouraging one another. There were multiple times when one of us would be struggling, and a letter would arrive unexpectedly at the perfect time to lift our spirits and change the course of our day or week. We built a spiritual connection first, and that led to a friendship and partnership destined to endure many struggles, frustrations, and heartaches.

When I was younger, I had a seemingly infinite number of choices for a spouse. I chose one who was resilient, fun-loving, gritty, spontaneous, spunky, and bold. She exhibited qualities that would push me to my limits of excellence later in life. Her outspoken courage has pushed me from one career advancement to the next. She doesn't let me be pushed around or manipulated, or allow the scheming, conniving, or ultra-ambitious to take advantage of me. She's a no-nonsense wife who keeps me in line and steers me out of potentially regressive situations and away from damning decisions. Back to the computer talk, my wife's like a firewall and antivirus software that keeps things running smoothly and protected from any malicious malware lurking in the shadows, looking for an opportunity to corrupt my system.

Accountability is another reason 1+1=3. Every day of success or failure directly impacts my wife and family. When I have someone counting on me, waiting for me to report to them each and every day, why would I daydream and dawdle or twiddle my thumbs rather than work my butt off? The worst thing in my wife's eyes is when I go to work and am away the whole day, leaving her alone with the kids, changing diapers, making meals, cleaning messes, folding laundry, and washing dishes, and then I come home and haven't sold a thing. If I haven't contributed to the success of my family at least as much as she did, then why was I gone at all? If I'm going to leave her alone to tend to the affairs of the home, then I better come back with something to show for it. I come home eager to report my successes because I know my wife expects daily progress and results. You can't buy that kind of accountability; it's the natural byproduct of the ever-advancing marriage relationship.

I strongly believe that marriage is an extremely important element to success through these principles. Throughout history, the most influential people almost always had a spouse to credit for a large part of their achievement. Even seemingly small things have had a huge impact on the course of history. Without Lillian Disney, Mickey Mouse would've been named Mortimer Mouse and it just wouldn't be the same. If you haven't had the opportunity to be married, you may not understand until you're in that role. The highlight of my day and my life is time spent with my family. Work is an important element of success; however, my greatest fulfillment comes when I'm teaching, nurturing, and striving to shape my family's dreams and goals into reality. The daily smiles and heartwarming laughter are irreplaceable ingredients in my life that I cherish more than any amount of money, fame, or recognition. In serving them, I find energy and strength beyond my own; drawing from their synergistic love, 1+1=3.

The $300K Homemaker

What does the wife of someone who is off-the-charts successful look like? First of all, she looks beautiful—at least, my wife does. Second of all, she's gritty. With all the stress and misery that we went through to get here, my wife has to be a special kind of crazy. Why didn't she leave me after our first summer selling alarms? Why didn't she leave me when we moved ten times in ten weeks? She went into our marriage expecting a plastic surgeon as a husband, and somehow, she got a door-to-door salesman. I remember we were at a party once, and someone asked me what I do for a living. I responded with a pretentious air of pride, "I'm in the marketing department for a home automation firm." My wife rolled her eyes and chimed in, "He sells security systems door-to-door." Her tone said, "Oh Josh, you're cute, let's just call it what it is; the prestige of becoming a surgeon is long gone." It's good to have someone around who is blunt and direct to humble you.

My wife is my most trusted advisor. She's my moral support. She's my VP.

My wife could do my job better than I can, guaranteed. I like her more than I like myself, so I know everyone else would too. Self-improvement is a major theme in our household. Our favorite literature is anything self-help related. Thanks to my wife, my children will be the beneficiaries of that attitude.

She knows she can make or break my success. A major part of accomplishing huge goals is having a positive attitude. A spouse can, in an instant, change your attitude about the day, week, month, year, or even life. You spend so much time with one individual who, sometimes unwittingly, holds your fate in their daily decision to be happy and supportive or angry and detractive. Due to that influence she carries, we've developed a synergy in our goals, and that is a massive component of how we've achieved so much together.

Writing this book was an example of how that synergy happened to me. I started dedicating fourteen to twenty-eight hours every week to writing. How would I have enough time to do that and run a sales team, while personally outselling everyone on my team? The next three chapters talk about that—somehow, the addition of more work made everything else I did more efficient, and I ended up having my best quarter ever. My experience makes me think that the jump from $30,000/year to $100,000/year is significantly tougher than the jump from $100,000/year to $300,000/year. Is that true about moving from $300,000/year to $1,000,000/year? That would be nice! I'll let you know. Most improvements in nature follow the Law of Diminishing Returns. There is a tapering or leveling off at some asymptotic limit of achievement. Income follows a different law, the Law of the Big MO. Increasing your speed and arriving at an ever-faster pace somehow makes life easier and makes the momentum you already built push you further and further toward your goals. Returns seem to snowball rather than diminish. Word of mouth and positive peer pressure drives more production and efficiency. My success and seeing that snowball has driven my wife to realize if her quirky husband can reach his crazy goals, then there's no reason she can't too. Success breeds success.

Newton's Third Law of Marriage

"For every action there is an equal and opposite reaction." My life tends to be happy and carefree right around the time when my wife is ready to flip out and vice versa. Somehow, one of us is usually the voice of reason and sanity when the other person is about to lose their mind. It sure is nice to have someone like that around to balance life out.

In Thomas J. Stanley's book, *The Millionaire Mind*, the research stems from a survey taken by hundreds of millionaires. The book attempts to discover and then paint a picture of how the wealthiest minds in America think. Stanley lists the top five elements of success that were given by that group of millionaires. In order, they are:

1. integrity
2. discipline
3. social skills
4. supportive spouse
5. hard work

From my experience, #4 on this list is vital to make #s 1, 2, 3, and 5 happen. When I want to be lazy, she reminds me to be disciplined; when I want to be antisocial, she encourages me to be excited and fun-loving around friends. As far as integrity is concerned, she keeps me 100-percent honest. She doesn't even have to say anything; just her involvement in my life keeps me accountable. "Would my wife approve?" is the question I constantly ask myself. If she wouldn't, then that means just don't do it! Having a supportive spouse is like having a second conscience: when the first one gives in to temptation, the second one slaps you and puts you back in place.

When a spouse is agreeing with your negativity rather than challenging it, or constantly complaining about life rather than seeking to improve it, success is short-lived. I've seen it so many times where the lack of a supportive spouse has derailed some people with the highest potential for success that I've ever known. If, by a small chance, you aren't a fully supportive spouse, I want you to take a minute to reflect and think about the impact you have on your significant other. Ask yourself the following questions:

1. Could I do better at helping my spouse reach all their dreams and goals?
2. Can I adjust my goals to support theirs?
3. Can I provide an equal and opposite reaction to challenge their negativity and push them to their limits of success?

I sure do love my wife, and I acknowledge that all my success has hinged on her willingness to support me. She's done a pretty fantastic job; I couldn't have asked for someone more perfect for me.

14 Treat the Company Like You Own It

A Whole New Attitude

A couple years ago, one of the regional vice presidents of my company interviewed me for a promotion to a management position. In the middle of that interview, he said something along the lines of, "I have to treat every decision I make as if this is MY company. I have to think, 'Who do I trust to hand over the keys to the Ferrari?'" Wow! To me, that was such a foreign and profound concept. Could you imagine the difference in culture of a company where every employee treated all their decisions with that level of ownership? I can definitely say that if I were writing the paychecks every single week, using my own bank account, I would make decisions differently. So, why not act that way regardless of who's writing the checks?

We recently had a sales rep leave our company who accidentally had been telling all his customers that an energy-efficiency audit wasn't required for their home. It absolutely is, though, because our company receives a rebate from the state of Connecticut worth 10 percent of the contract value. To skip that simple audit repeatedly over time would literally cost our company millions of dollars in lost revenue. Making exceptions for extenuating circumstances is a slippery slope that if you aren't careful can turn into a wasteful habit. There were a number of escalated customers who didn't want to get that audit done, and as a result, I received an email asking me if we should just skip it for those customers and not receive the state rebate. The easiest route would've been to skip it and move on. The ownership mentality I've tried to adopt replied with a resounding, "Absolutely not!" There was no question in my mind that we needed to resolve the situation in a way that included getting that rebate.

Businesses have two main numbers they're always focused on improving: revenue and the company's bottom-line profit, commonly known as earnings. Performance in these metrics are fundamental in how Wall Street determines valuation. These numbers are what makes or breaks any company's stock price. If you skip something that greatly impacts both of those numbers and is so simple to complete (like an energy audit) just because it's inconvenient, then you definitely don't deserve the keys to the Ferrari. If a company announces their earnings each quarter and they do better than what the analysts expected on both of those metrics, revenue and profit, that's when stock prices soar. The better those numbers, the better the employees are at adopting the ownership mentality.

This leads to the question, "If you were the owner of the company, what should you know that you haven't learned yet?" As an example, do you understand accounting and finance? Do you complain every time you request something and it gets denied because "the finance team didn't approve it," or do you think, "Thank goodness that went by the finance team before we moved forward?" Is your level of understanding of finance and accounting strong enough that you would be confident in fulfilling your job description with an ownership mentality?

While I was in college, I finished my chemistry degree requirements a year and a half ahead of schedule (not because I'm smart but because I decided to switch from a BS to a BA degree, which required way less time to complete). With this gift of extra time, I had to decide what would be the most useful classes for my future. I ended up making one of the best decisions of my educational career. I decided to get two minors:

1. Finance: which consisted of classes in sales, marketing, accounting, economics, and finance
2. Spanish: which drastically helped improve my fluency in the Spanish language

I specifically chose classes that I knew would make me more valuable and increase my knowledge of how the world operates. I had already taken the tough chemistry classes and proven my grit and ability to take on huge challenges. Now it was time to learn the most practical and relevant information for my career. Those classes were the easiest ones I took throughout my four years in college, but the knowledge I gleaned from them was the most pertinent to my success in the business world. Everything else being equal, would you rather hire the chemist or teacher or artist or actor or writer or architect or doctor or lawyer, etc. who understands finance and speaks another language, or the one who just knows their subject? To maximize the value you bring to a company, you need to maximize revenue and profit. Think of your job: do you do that? Are you showing ownership and learning how the whole business operates? There are so many businesses that flop. I'm willing to bet that has something to do with a lack of financial knowledge among the employees, and the owners, for that matter.

As a result of the habits I developed in my finance classes, I now get daily news alerts from Google that give me an update on my company and industry. I'm reading dozens of research and opinion articles every week that talk about the trends in the market. Consumer demand has shifted several times in the past decade, and as a result, our company has made several difficult policy and directional adjustments to remain sustainable and successful long term. I'm always anticipating changes, and when the company makes decisions I don't fully agree with, I try to understand how and why it would make sense. While I don't recommend following blindly, even if you don't agree 100 percent with company changes, again think, "If this were my company, how would I want myself to respond?"

The last questions that I want to pose to help you develop this new attitude of ownership are these: Do you speak of your job as if you are the CEO, always improving the public image? Or are you a cancer in your company, constantly bringing it down with every word out of your mouth? Do you publicly resist and backbite the leadership? Or do you verbally support those chosen to lead the charge to success? You have to always remember to speak positively about the company . . . especially to your wife! Telling your spouse something bad about your company can be just as detrimental as telling your parent something bad about your spouse. I received sage advice a couple weeks before I was married: "Never tell your parents anything negative about your wife; you'll forget about it in a day or a week, but your parent will never forget, even long after the issue gets resolved." Speaking ill of the company you work for to your wife or anyone else, for that matter, will continue to bring down your company's reputation long after you have overcome your personal issues.

This attitude is vital because in every interaction you have with a client, they will be able to tell if you're confident in the mission and direction of your business or if you're leaving to a competitor in the next few months. People are hesitant to work with the uncommitted sales person . . . and owners are typically the last ones to leave their own business.

Ownership versus Renting

Why is it that when you're renting just about anything, it's 100 times more likely to get trashed or abused? Think about it: would you ever want to buy a rental car after thousands of different drivers drove the car while pretending to be street racers in *The Fast and the Furious*? Fast acceleration, sudden braking, and multiple drivers are some of the quickest ways to destroy a car. The different driving styles and habits wear down the tires, steering, brakes, transmission, even the audio system, and just about every component way quicker.

What about buying a house that was a rental for decades? Rental homes seem to only get deep cleaned at most once a year, when someone is moving out/in. There's no incentive to take care of the walls, doors, carpet, appliances, plumbing, electrical, or anything. You're just paying to use the property for a limited time; your check isn't paying for even a small chunk of equity and ownership each month. The currency digits in your bank account leave, never to be seen again. What's the point in taking care of something you'll never see again? The worst the landlord can do is keep your deposit, so who cares?

Now contrast that with ownership. Since we bought our first home almost a year ago, my wife and I have gradually made it better than we found it. We've made both little and big improvements here and there almost every single week. We've changed carpet, updated light switches, painted, removed old stickers on the windows, added solar lights in the yard, trimmed trees that were hitting the house, sealed all the drafts in the doors and windows, swapped out light bulbs for more efficient ones, and bought a new, more efficient washer and dryer. The list is growing constantly. Our surroundings are continually improving, whereas in our apartments, it seemed like things got worse the longer we stayed there. We relied on the landlord to fix everything, and we weren't about to invest too much time on something we would only use temporarily.

This idea is a metaphor for your company. If you aren't self-employed, then technically you're renting your job and income from someone else. What can you do to stop renting?

Because my company is publicly traded, I was able to buy stock in it. I literally bought a piece of the company. If the company succeeds, then my stock is worth more. If I help my company beat market expectations and succeed at high levels, then I directly benefit. I recommend not being too heavily invested in your company, though, because if the company goes bankrupt, you don't want your entire income *and* net worth to disappear in an instant. However, I do think it's important to have at least a portion of your net worth that is dependent on the success or failure of your business. This extrinsic motivation for making good decisions, coupled with the intrinsic desire for your company's success, is a recipe for big results.

Another thing I did to increase ownership was choosing to manage a sales team. I set a goal to very quickly get promoted into a management position because I would have a vested interest in the success of a larger body. My pay is, in part, directly based on the success of a multimillion-dollar branch of the company. This has made it so I have equity in another chunk of the company; again, just like stock, I literally have ownership in the company. I think it's essential for that pay to become aligned with the success of the company in order to achieve the attitude of ownership. Without this alignment, you're just renting your job, and like renting an apartment, you can walk away at any point, throwing away your momentum, your stability, and your time.

Lastly, recruiting and building the company also naturally evokes the ownership mentality. When you recruit and hire a friend, you have to sell them on why they should work with you and your company. Once you hire them, they're depending on you to show them that you and your company were the right choice. You have someone depending on you for their livelihood. That pressure and their high expectations makes me want to deliver and not disappoint. I feel like I'm being watched and held to a higher standard by those recruits. I can never waiver in my confidence about the company—*my* company. At my company, when a recruit is successful, I get a pay increase. The more value you add, the more you have to be compensated; if that isn't the case, your company needs to change, or you need to change companies to one you can own.

The Human Billboard

This section applies to you whether you actually own your business or not. Everywhere I go, I'm a walking, talking, driving advertisement for my company. My personal car is wrapped with vinyl lettering to promote the company. It doesn't matter where I go, I'm the guy who drives the "cute" tiny solar car. I often point to my car and ask my new customers, "You've probably seen the tiny car around the area?" They will respond and say, "Yeah, I've seen those solar smart cars all over the place!" I'm the only one in the entire state with a car like mine. They've seen the same car driving around everywhere, zipping around from appointment to appointment. This self-imposed branding has more than recouped the $250 cost to wrap the vehicle, and it's also returned substantially more than the $10,000 that I spent to buy the car.

In most cases, the more familiar a brand is, the easier it is for people to buy. McDonald's has the familiar golden arches that are seen at what seems like every highway exit. That's how they have over $25,000,000,000 in sales every year! My goal for my sales territory is to make my business and brand as recognizable as the McDonald's arches. I want to flood my relatively small geographic market with advertising. My wrapped car has been the best way to do that. If I'm seen zipping around town every day, that means business is booming. If business is booming, that means I probably have something they should want.

Another way to subtly increase brand recognition is with swag. If used properly, swag can be awesome for branding. There's something unique about my company's culture: I wear a Vivint polo shirt while I'm working, and when I get home, I change into a Vivint t-shirt.

My company has been a fantastic example of applying the human billboard principle. They went as far as spending millions of dollars to buy the naming rights to a professional sports arena. For the next decade, any time the Utah Jazz plays a home game, the millions of fans from both teams will see the name *"Vivint Smart Home Arena,"* and my brand will become a little more familiar nationwide. While that marketing was done on a large scale, reaching millions, my job is to focus on my target market, which consists of a town of only 60,000 people. Everyone in my town needs to see the company name so when I stop by their home or their friend refers them, they have already been exposed to my brand. Credibility is already established. The customer is warmer to the idea of buying from me because chances are that if they've seen my company name before, it means someone else is probably buying from my company. They naturally think there probably isn't much risk if they buy too. The buying pressure is relieved—or at least, lessened—before I even talk to them. My interaction with the customer changes from selling and convincing to teaching, clarifying, and filling out a little bit of paperwork. This is a prime example of how the Jones Effect works.

Another example of the human billboard principle comes from my wife. She recently started a business selling a lipstick product that lasts for upward of eighteen hours. She's done an awesome job so far, selling thousands of dollars' worth in a relatively short period of time. She applied this human billboard principle in a few different ways. First of all, she wears her lipstick day and night because she absolutely loves it. She always looks like she's ready to go somewhere important; it doesn't matter if she's going to the gym or grocery shopping or just vegetating at home, she looks like a model ready to audition for a CoverGirl commercial.

The next thing she did was start a Facebook group, where she started doing daily Facebook Live videos, regular giveaways, and a never-ending barrage of social media games. She makes sure she wears her lipstick or mentions it in every single video and post she does on social media.

On top of that, she also started putting lipstick color stripes on the back of her hand. That made it so people would ask her what she had on her hand. It made it so easy to start talking about her product to random strangers and good friends alike because they were curious about the rainbow of colors conveniently placed in plain sight.

The last thing my wife did was buy a t-shirt that said, "Ask me about my lipstick." She literally became a billboard encouraging people to buy her product. She hasn't talked to me about wrapping her car to look like a giant tube of Pink Champagne lipstick, but I sense that's coming soon.

Integrity

In Thomas J. Stanley's book, *The Millionaire Mind*, integrity was ranked as the top reason to which millionaires attribute their success. I likewise attribute a large part of my success to integrity. This is one quality or characteristic that should never be compromised or ignored.

If you steal from the company, you're only stealing from yourself. If you cheat or lie to a customer, you're only costing yourself future business and maybe even your job. If you're honest, no one usually thinks twice about it because that's how you should be anyway. However, if you're dishonest, everyone in the world is going to hear about it. Angry customers are going to post that negative experience on social media, yelp, Google reviews, Consumer Affairs, and every outlet they can think of. If they're talking with friends, they'll tell them to avoid your business like the plague.

Negative reviews are easy to come by: just blatantly lie to someone, and it'll probably show up the next day. Positive reviews, on the other hand, have to be earned by going above and beyond the norm. If you put in the extra effort to get them, they're like gold to your business.

I noticed a huge improvement in my sales closing percentage from 2015 to 2016. I attribute that in large part to my efforts in 2015 to build solid relationships with customers and then ask them to leave reviews for our company. In my office, I've personally generated four times as many positive reviews as the next highest person because I asked ten times as many people to leave a review. The majority of the reviews from other reps is due to me pushing the other reps to ask their customers to leave positive feedback. In 2015, I noticed that many of my customers cited negative reviews as the main reason they cancelled moving forward with our services. I decided to put an end to that miserable trend that made me feel powerless. We are a multimillion-dollar local branch that's part of a multibillion-dollar national company. I don't want the mistakes or dishonesty of a handful of reps who live on the other side of the country and don't even work for my company anymore to be the reason my name and my brand is tarnished. To fix it, I worked like crazy to generate a significant number of positive reviews for my location specifically. This made it so I could show my customers the feedback and testimonials from their neighbors before they even looked up reviews. I know they're going to look us up because I do the exact same thing when I'm shopping around for services! Reviews are an instant barometer of a business' integrity. This is shown in the following statistics found in the Local Consumer Review Survey 2016 conducted by Bright Local[35]:

- 84 percent of people trust online reviews as much as a personal recommendation.
- 7 out of 10 consumers will leave a review for a business if they're asked to.

---

[35]"Local Consumer Review Survey, BrightLocal, BrightLocal Ltd., accessed 17 October 2017, https://www.brightlocal.com/learn/local-consumer-review-survey/.

- 90 percent of consumers read fewer than ten reviews before forming an opinion about a business.
- 54 percent of people will visit the website after reading positive reviews.
- 73 percent of consumers think that reviews older than three months are no longer relevant.
- 74 percent of consumers say that positive reviews make them trust a local business more.
- 58 percent of consumers say that the star rating of a business is most important.

What happens if I or one of my sales reps lies to a customer and they publish that negative review? It'll take a lot of explaining to resolve that concern, or in most cases, it may never be resolved. Look at those statistics! If you're ignoring your online reviews, then your business will absolutely suffer in this age of technology. Lies come back to haunt you a lot easier in the digital age.

It's a common misconception that you have to lie to be successful at sales. In fact, the opposite is true. The dishonest salesperson is forced to pick up and move because he can't stay in the same place too long. They are the "magic" tonic peddlers who get run out of the village after people realize the fraud has been selling snake oil or dirty water with giardia. They live off of today and don't plan for the future. Conversely, a reputable brand is built off of years of integrity and trust.

My personal favorite thing to see in a review is something like: "They made a mistake, but they fixed it right away!" That's a perfect review for showing integrity. To err is human nature. We need to accept those weaknesses; however, when they negatively impact others, we need to make restitution. Own the mistake and fix it! I recently had my oil changed; as a courtesy, they also topped off all the other fluids in the car. Somehow, the mechanic accidentally forgot to replace the coolant reservoir cap. This occurred in the middle of winter on one of the coldest days of the year. I didn't notice anything was wrong until my heater suddenly stopped heating and my windows wouldn't defog. I slowly drove to the nearest store to buy more antifreeze; I had to drive with the windows down while wiping the windshield to be able to see. I ended up losing the majority of my antifreeze, and so I had to buy a brand-new gallon of it. I went back to the shop where they had changed my oil, and they inspected the car to make sure there was no harm done to the radiator. They then asked me how much the antifreeze cost. I said it was around $5. They gave me a $10 bill and said sorry. The look in their eyes was one of sincere regret and integrity. That extra $5 was a simple yet powerful symbol of their goal to perform honest labor to earn an honest living. They should sleep well at night with their level of integrity. I kept that $10 on the dashboard of my car for about a year to remind me about my goal of perfect integrity. Whenever I need my oil changed in the future, that little shop will be my first choice for life.

I initially chose to get my oil changed at that mechanic shop because of specific reviews that referenced their honesty, as well as their integrity by sharing the longevity of their repeat business. I read these reviews and was immediately sold. I consequently had my own experience that tested their integrity, and as you saw, they passed with flying colors. In my business, I strive to emulate the honesty of the team at JP Automotive.

Like I said earlier, if you cheat or lie, you're only shooting yourself in the foot. What happens if a mechanic at that shop starts to tell people little fibs, like they need new brakes or new tires prematurely, and people start to uncover the truth? Well, his business will get some negative reviews. So what? He's paid hourly, he still makes the same amount of money, right? Wrong. Fewer customers means less productivity and slower work days, which means each employee's value as an hourly worker just went down. If a mechanic is sitting around waiting for customers to show up rather than doing revenue-generating work, that means the owner will either need to cut pay or lay off someone. Who's going to get booted first? The person who generated those negative reviews that lost business in the first place. Treat the company like you're the one writing the paychecks every week. Treat your customers like they're paying you directly for the service. Perform the quality of work that you would want performed if you were the one who had to take money directly out of your wallet to fix any mistakes or oversights.

This idea of integrity extends not only to your customers, but it also includes your coworkers, employees, and superiors. Who wants to work with a pathological liar? I've worked with them and it's not fun. *The Speed of Trust* by Stephen M. R. Covey talks about how we are slower to achieve when there is no foundation of trust. When you can't trust anything someone says, it's difficult to delegate any responsibility to them because you never know if it will happen. When someone lies once, I want to fire them. Even seemingly small things, like running late for a meeting, drives me crazy . . . but only if they lie about it. Just own up to what you did wrong, if you're late, then maybe you didn't set your alarm clock for an appropriate time to leave your house soon enough, maybe you didn't factor in traffic—just call it how it is!

Improving reviews through a dedication to honesty is one of the most valuable long-term actions anyone can do for their company. For my industry specifically, these reviews take years to build up. In order to get meaningful reviews, it requires a great deal of trust from the customer because they are essentially a cosigner on the integrity of your business. They're signing their name next to yours, basically saying, "They're good for what they promised." This trust and faith in my company is built during a lengthy sales process that takes six to eight months. Keeping someone happy for that long takes dedication and extreme patience. How many people do you know that you would cosign with them for a loan? You have to really trust someone, trust that they'll keep their promise to deliver, to pay their bills. Even if they're family members or close friends, it doesn't mean you want to sign your name beneath theirs confirming, backing up, or ultimately being held responsible for their integrity. Getting a positive review is no different than winning the trust of a co-signer on a business loan.

The bottom line is that perfect integrity will pay dividends for decades to come. Your reputation will precede you and the speed of your business's sales will accelerate faster than you can possibly imagine. Nice guys don't finish last.

15 Self-Discipline: The Time I Almost Bought a Tesla for $85K and Lost My $1K Deposit.

Kronk

Unfortunately, making good and sometimes difficult decisions today makes life exponentially better years down the road. Compounding interest really is the eighth wonder of the world. If you take $60,000 a year and put it into a fund earning 6 percent interest, then you will make an extra $20,000 a year . . . after ten years. The first year, it's only $3,600 but it grows and multiplies. Twenty years is better than ten and thirty is better than twenty. That's why wrinkly old Warren Buffet is loaded. Doodads are so tempting. Don't do it! Delay your gratification; if you wait and invest your money, you can get whatever you want, plus a little extra, for free! Increasing your income doesn't mean you have to or even should increase your consumption habits. If you almost feel obligated to spend and consume more when you earn more, don't.

In *The Power of Ambition*, Jim Rohn said, "An immediate reward for lack of discipline is a fun day at the beach . . . a future reward of discipline is owning the beach. For most we choose today's pleasure over tomorrow's fortune."[36]

---

[36]John Rohn, *The Power of Ambition*, narrated by John Rohn (Nightingale-Conant Corporation, 1994).

Oh, how it would be nice to be ignorant of these principles; I would be significantly more gratified right now. I guess I've read too many self-help books for my own good.

I feel like I had one of the most defining moments of my life just the other week. I was in such a crazy emotional and financial tug of war. I felt like the character Kronk from the Disney cartoon *The Emperor's New Groove*.

Image 16: Angel vs devil

The devil car I wanted to buy said, "Look what I can do," and my wife, the angel who was supposed to help me resist the temptation, said, "He has a point." She almost wanted the car for me more than I wanted it for myself. Autopilot, all-wheel drive, electric, crazy-fast acceleration, beautiful sound system, flawless exterior design, winter weather package, all-glass panoramic moonroof, the perfect color, alas. I was so close to buying my dream car, but I stopped before it was too late, and I'm so glad I didn't give in.

Spiritual Discipline

I had just started reading *The Millionaire Next Door* right before I made the decision not to buy that stupid, beautiful car. That book changed my whole perception of finances; it was absolutely fantastic. It really drove home the notion of delayed or even indefinitely resisted gratification. While reading it, I realized that some Biblical teachings have helped me throughout my life to adopt those principles. In my religious practices, there are multiple ways that I've been taught this idea. Fasting is one of the most difficult things I *attempt* to do on a monthly basis. I absolutely love to eat; I eat five to six times a day and have become somewhat of a foodie over the years. Fasting involves abstaining from food and drink for a twenty-four-hour period. Yikes! It's a tough practice that really teaches self-control and discipline; it teaches us to put off the "natural man," the gluttonous person who only wants to consume. Fasting really challenges how deeply you're committed to your purpose, but if successful, it ultimately reaffirms to the body that the mind is the master. With that physical sacrifice, you also take the money that you would've spent on food during those twenty-four hours and donate it to the poor and less fortunate. The key word here is "sacrifice." That sacrifice brings a renewed sense of gratitude for health, strength, and food, that makes me personally more focused on not taking any day for granted. I choose to live every day more focused on achieving my goals because I know I've been blessed with a capable mind and body, able to perform at a level higher than 99 percent of the world. Many, many people have my same capability to perform at that level, but lack the discipline to just put their head down and get stuff done.

Another way I've learned stronger self-discipline and gratitude is through an ancient Hebrew law known as tithing. Tithing is the practice of donating one-tenth of your "annual increase" to the church, or more accurately, to God. Once a year in our church, we meet with the leader of our congregation to discuss our financial contributions, and we "declare" whether or not we paid the full 10 percent. This past year, our church leader had us read the following scripture in the Old Testament book of Malachi:

> Bring ye all the tithes into the storehouse, that there may be meat in mine house, and prove me now herewith, saith the Lord of hosts, if I will not open you the windows of heaven, and pour you out a blessing, that there shall not be room enough to receive it.

> And I will rebuke the devourer for your sakes, and he shall not destroy the fruits of your ground; neither shall your vine cast her fruit before the time in the field, saith the Lord of hosts.[37]

The follow-up question we were asked was, "What does the 'devourer' mean to you?" I gave some generic obvious answer. My wife then thoughtfully responded that the "devourer" is the consumer, the natural man or woman who wants instant gratification and wants to buy everything in sight—the shopaholic, the tv addict, the couch potato, the sloth. A blessing or natural result of tithing is the willpower to have the inner devourer rebuked and have your wealth, or the "fruits of your ground," preserved. That response rang true and made me reflect on my inner "devourer."

After pondering on that conversation, I reflected on my life and realized the profound impact that these principles have had on my success. Both the ideas

---

[37]Mal. 3:10–11

of tithing and fasting, along with many others, have helped me to live within a budget and always spend way less than what I bring in. Why is this important? Why is having the self-control to live within or below your means important for the overall theme of soaring to the top of the income percentile curve? I can tell you from sad personal experience that this notion of modest spending has been absolutely critical to my success; the next section explains how. It illustrates an example of a time I made one small mistake and didn't live within my means, and I consequently failed to rise above a mediocre performance at my job.

You Never Want to Write This Letter

One dreadful year during summer sales, my expenses were more than what I brought in each week. I was carpooling with my best friend to my work area, and on our way out, we stopped at a gas station to fill up. I went to swipe my card to pitch in my fair share of gas money. My bank card was rejected. My credit card, which was already almost maxed out, had just had "fraudulent activity" reported on it, so they were sending me a new one. My net worth was literally negative; my self-worth felt even lower. I didn't even have enough money to chip in to carpool to work. How do you think I felt trying to sell my product and convince other people to spend money when I couldn't even pay for $6 of gas? I vividly remember my desperation that day in Beaumont, Texas. I remember someone telling me they weren't interested in the alarm system I was "peddling," and I felt my eyes unexpectedly well up with tears. After that rejection, the only thought I had was that, because that person told me "no," I wouldn't make any money to feed my family.

I went home that night and wrote the following email to my sales manager:

> Hey Scott,
> My problems and frustrations are nothing compared to what you're probably going through. I've been super stressed too, but I haven't really thought I was validated in complaining to anyone because everyone else is probably going through something similar.
>
> I haven't been selling, and so I don't have money to pay for my liabilities. That gets me more stressed, and so I can't sell, and it's just a spiraling down effect. I've had a couple times where I almost started crying on a doorstep, pretty pathetic huh?
>
> My wife just said we really need you here. I also need Brock here, he's been sucking way bad too. I get my energy and motivation from the people around me. You two are the ones who got me excited about working with this team and for Vivint. Even though I think you are insane at times, you get people pumped around you to go out and work.

I really wouldn't have any problems if it weren't for the abnormal number of cancels that I've had this year. It's been about 15% of my jobs have canceled after it's installed including that one in Amarillo that the tech was late to. I had three of those happen in the same week, and that was really what made me start worrying. To top it all off this year hasn't been ideal because we've been moving around living in hotels that aren't meant to healthily sustain life. My wife and I are typically extremely healthy people, but we've been living off of junk that is cooked in the microwave because that's all we have. As a result, I don't have any energy because my body isn't receiving nutrients. Additionally, right before we left Wyoming my daughter started sleeping through the night, but because she probably feels insecure she hasn't been doing so well since we started; I've had one night of decent sleep since I've been out here. I know now why you didn't have your family come out.

Since we're eating out and traveling so much, I've spent so much more money than anticipated. Our rent in Wyoming isn't that bad, it's only $650/month, but when I only sell 5 in a week and then 3 cancel and then $275 is taken out for rent, I'm really only making enough to feed my family. We were spending over $100 a week in Wyoming with a kitchen stocked full of everything we need, making food from scratch. It's a lot more expensive to live out of a hotel. You know that.

I don't like asking people for help because it makes me seem desperate, weak, or irresponsible. I thought, however, there might be some flexibility with the rent that is charged, because I know we're going to be reimbursed for almost half of it at the end of the summer. It was just a thought I had because this has been a big struggle for me for the last few weeks and I'm just looking at all my options to be able to afford my expenses. I haven't been mentally tough and selling because I'm financially distressed at the moment. As soon as I figure this out I'll be able to better handle the other stresses we have.

I loved working with the team last year and I loved it this year up until we left Amarillo. I was ready to sell 150, and it looked like I was on target to do it. That seems so far away when my biggest concern is how to pay for my expenses. I just need to get kicked back into gear. It feels like I should be one of the top people in the office, but it seems like I'm getting further and further from that point.

I know it's been hard for everyone; these circumstances are beyond anyone's control. It hasn't been ideal for a single person out here. I'm not complaining or saying you've done anything wrong, I just wanted you to have the background for why I was asking for help.

Thanks.

Thanks, Scott—you'll never realize the impact and tremendous influence you had in shaping my life.

I still cringe and have flashbacks to those heavy moments of desperation when I go back and read that email. It's really humbling when you have to write a letter like that. That feeling of being locked in a downward spiral was so miserable. I was drowning and needed some kind of a win just to feel like I could stay afloat. I was stressed about being broke, and that stress made it harder to be successful at work, which made me have even less money, and the vicious cycle repeated till I finally hit my breaking point. I have so much gratitude for the people who helped me that summer; they saw my potential and had confidence in me. They gave me a special exception for rent, and that, in turn, made it so I had just enough income to work for the rest of the summer. My level of success improved, and I finally made it out of the financial pit I had found myself in. Interestingly enough, three months before this experience where I found myself forced to write that email, my wife and I had taken out a loan for an $18,000 car. It seemed easily affordable based on what I expected myself to earn that coming summer. Plans and reality often differ. Lesson learned: don't make large purchases based on income expectations. The thought I had this time around with the $85,000 car was, "I made 300-flipping-thousand dollars in a year, why not reward myself with a car where the payments would only cost me 5 percent of my yearly income?!" You'll see in a just a bit why that thought was so self-deceiving.

Removing and preventing financial stress lets your mind focus on the most important tasks at hand rather than dwelling on the thought, "How do I get myself out of this mess?"

Don't Work for Money

Let's contrast that summer, when I had to write that painful letter, with my first year working at my current job. At the end of my last summer selling alarms, I received a paycheck for a little less than half of my total earnings in one lump sum. It was what's called a "backend check," and mine was about $35,000. That was equal to about seven months of living expenses for my family; as a result, I started my new job without a single financial care. What a difference that made! I didn't think about money when talking to any of my customers. I literally didn't care if they said yes or no. The purpose of my work wasn't for me to make money; my purpose was to help people get an awesome product that didn't cost them anything and would save them money. Work no longer felt like work. I loved the skeptical yet excited expression on people's faces when they say, "You mean it doesn't cost anything?"

Money often clouds our heartfelt intentions. Mark Twain had it right when he said, "The lack of money is the root of all evil." I've seen how having more money can set us free from a shroud of cloudiness. However, in order to best utilize our excess income, "disposable" income can't be seen and used as if it were disposable; it has to be used in part as a consecrated financial reserve. If an individual has multiple years of life expenses in the bank, then from my personal experience, intentions can be more pure, more selfless. No one should have to work for money; I think that it often breeds dishonesty, corruption, and fraud. If your heart is set on making more money, then that greed or intention will be made manifest in your attitude and actions toward others. If someone tells you "no," or, "I don't want your product," what's your reaction? Do you get angry? Do you turn into a completely different person? Was the friendly smile and the courtesy all just a show so you can make money? I was a slave to money for that summer when I overextended myself financially. There was a distinct difference in how I felt and performed once I finally had more than what I needed. I didn't depend on a green piece of paper, and I was free to focus on just helping people. I imagine that dependence on money is how a drug addict must feel, always needing more just to feel normal. Learn from my mistake. Don't abuse money. If it's abused like a drug, then you'll get similarly destructive results. Getting high on heroin every day to gratify yourself will destroy your life; however, having a few doses of morphine the day of an appendectomy will certainly make life more pleasant. So it is with money.

Let's return back to the subtitle of the chapter: "The Time I Almost Bought a Tesla for $85K and Lost My $1K Deposit." What a miserable experience. I was in a vicious tug of war between my short-term and long-term wants. In the short term, I wanted a beautiful car with incredible features that would make any car enthusiast drool with unquenchable lust. In the long term, I wanted to provide a sustainable, secure, and comfortable life for my family. One of my future goals is to have enough money saved and invested so that a decade from now, I don't have to work for money ever again. My basic living expenses will be covered for life. The title of the book I'll write then will be, *Set for Life @ 36*. With that kind of financial security, could you imagine the internal peace? What would you do with your life if you didn't need money? Would you run for a political office? Would you become an actor? Maybe a model? Would you travel more? Would you start a nonprofit charity? Would you do missionary work? Would you take a nap every day? Would you write a book? Would you race motorcycles? Would you take time to finally grow an organic vegetable garden? What would you do if money weren't an obstacle, but instead, provided you with unlimited freedom to pursue your passions?

Robert D. Hales of The Church of Jesus Christ of Latter-Day Saints gave an excellent talk called, "Becoming Provident Providers Temporally and Spiritually." This is an excerpt from that talk with two anecdotes that summarize this whole notion of provident living:

> *Being provident providers, we must keep that most basic commandment, "Thou shalt not covet" (Exodus 20:17). Our world is fraught with feelings of entitlement. Some of us feel embarrassed, ashamed, less*

worthwhile if our family does not have everything the neighbors have. As a result, we go into debt to buy things we can't afford—and things we do not really need. Whenever we do this, we become poor temporally and spiritually. We give away some of our precious, priceless agency and put ourselves in self-imposed servitude. Money we could have used to care for ourselves and others must now be used to pay our debts. What remains is often only enough to meet our most basic physical needs. Living at the subsistence level, we become depressed, our self-worth is affected, and our relationships with family, friends, neighbors, and the Lord are weakened. We do not have the time, energy, or interest to seek spiritual things.

How then do we avoid and overcome the patterns of debt and addiction to temporal, worldly things? May I share with you two lessons in provident living that can help each of us. These lessons, along with many other important lessons of my life, were taught to me by my wife and eternal companion. These lessons were learned at two different times in our marriage—both on occasions when I wanted to buy her a special gift.

The first lesson was learned when we were newly married and had very little money. I was in the air force, and we had missed Christmas together. I was on assignment overseas. When I got home, I saw a beautiful dress in a store window and suggested to my wife that if she liked it, we would buy it. Mary went into the dressing room of the store. After a moment the sales clerk came out, brushed by me, and returned the dress to its place in the store window. As we left the store, I asked, "What happened?" She replied, "It was a beautiful dress, but we can't afford it!" Those words went straight to my heart. I have learned that the three most loving words are "I love you," and the four most caring words for those we love are "We can't afford it."

The second lesson was learned several years later when we were more financially secure. Our wedding anniversary was approaching, and I wanted to buy Mary a fancy coat to show my love and appreciation for our many happy years together. When I asked what she thought of the coat I had in mind, she replied with words that again penetrated my heart and mind. "Where would I wear it?" she asked. (At the time she was a ward Relief Society president helping to minister to needy families.)

Then she taught me an unforgettable lesson. She looked me in the eyes and sweetly asked, "Are you buying this for me or for you?" In other words, she was asking, "Is the purpose of this gift to show your love for me or to show me that you are a good provider or to prove something to the world?" I pondered her question and realized I was thinking less about her and our family and more about me.

After that we had a serious, life-changing discussion about provident living, and both of us agreed that our money would be better spent in paying down our home mortgage and adding to our children's education fund.

These two lessons are the essence of provident living. When faced with the choice to buy, consume, or engage in worldly things and activities, we all need to learn to say to one another, "We can't afford it, even though we want it!" or "We can afford it, but we don't need it—and we really don't even want it!"[38]

For me, this was one of the most painful lessons to experience. I felt my pride being broken down during the tug of war over whether to buy that car. I could've easily afforded that car. I, however, could not afford the long-term negative impact it would've had on my goals. I put $1,000 down on the car that I'll never see again, but the lesson I learned from the ordeal is worth 1,000 times what I lost. (Update: I later disputed the charge and got my money back. Thank you, Amex!) Future successes are much easier when you accrue more than is needed and save up for that unexpected rainy day. Would I love to be driving a Tesla right now? Absolutely! Would I feel like I betrayed myself by succumbing to my pride? Probably . . . I may one day indulge myself, but that day doesn't feel too terribly close. I won't spend hard-earned money on it, though; I'll be sure to pay for my luxury with money earned from passive income generated by my investments.

Millionaire Math

To quote him again, Winston Churchill was famous for saying, "The farther back you can look, the farther forward you are likely to see." Decisions need to be made now based on what will happen decades later as a result of those decisions. Looking years into the past allows us to fully see the compound effect in action. Studying our own history or the history of others enables us to see how one misguided step destroyed our opportunities decades later, and conversely, it shows us how one wise action led individuals to create legacies, inspire the masses, or discover a secret that led to massive success.

There are two types of millionaire attitudes, young money and old money. Frivolity characterizes the young money, whereas longevity and lasting value follows the old money mentality. Young money is embodied in the NBA player who goes broke after making tens of millions of dollars. There are many examples of professional athletes who have thrown their wealth away from lavish spending, buying mansions, yachts, jets, thousands of shoes, and giant fish tanks. Other contributing

---

[38]Elder Robert D. Hales, "Becoming Provident Providers Temporally and Spiritually" (speech, Salt Lake City, Utah, April 2009), The Church of Jesus Christ of Latter-Day Saints: General Conference, https://www.lds.org/general-conference/2009/04/becoming-provident-providers-temporally-and-spiritually?lang=eng.

factors were vices like gambling, alcohol, excessive spending on car addictions for themselves and multiple family members, and ultimately, divorce settlements followed up with exorbitant child support payments. To contrast that, the old money mentality is embodied in the investor who owns various income-producing pieces of real estate, farmland, stocks, bonds, gold, fine art, and a handful of businesses. The typical member of this group drives a modest car and lives in a modest home. Read *The Millionaire Next Door*, and you'll get a taste of that concept. The media portrays a distorted view of wealth; somehow, frivolous spending is synonymous with wealth. That's an incorrect representation of the "old money" category. Rather than wasting and spending their life's work on depreciable assets, they earn, retain, and grow their wealth. Learn from the past mistakes of your predecessors. Study history, especially from a financial perspective. Adopt the good, shun the bad, and consequently, your future will be brighter than others' past.

This old money idea is so difficult to adopt, though! Every day, I see beautiful cars all around me that I could probably better afford than the people driving them can. I have to learn humility every day. While I was serving that two-year mission for my church, the president of the mission, John Darrington, told me to take this passage from the Book of Mormon to heart:

> And now I would that ye should be humble, and be submissive and gentle; easy to be entreated; full of patience and long-suffering; being temperate in all things; being diligent in keeping the commandments of God at all times; asking for whatsoever things ye stand in need, both spiritual and temporal; always returning thanks unto God for whatsoever things ye do receive.[39]

This verse pretty much sums up my Tesla temptation. I have so much to be grateful for. I don't need my pride to be gratified. "Full of patience and long-suffering"—I don't know how anyone can like the sound of that phrase, but I do know that in order to achieve long-term and lasting wealth accumulation, it's necessary to save and invest, rather than spend and consume. That car would realistically cost me more than double the $85,000 sticker price. The following numbers will make you change the way you think about spending; I got the idea to calculate this while I was reading *The Millionaire Next Door*, trying to decide if I should give in to my temptation. This may be one of the most fascinating thoughts I've pieced together. Pay very close attention; this is the way millionaires do math when they make a purchase:

$85,000 car
-$7,500 tax credit
=$77,500
+$15,000 in interest.
=$92,500

---

[39]Alma 7:23

Now, what is the pre-tax amount of earned income needed to make that purchase? Meaning, how much money did you need to earn before you paid your taxes in order to make a $92,500 purchase? Assuming an ultra-conservative 25 percent income tax rate, here's how to do that math:

$92,500/.75
= $123,333

This is pre-tax dollars I would have needed to earn in order to buy that car. I also donate 10 percent of my income to my church, so pre-donation dollars would be a factor as well to get exact numbers.

$123,333/.90
= $137,036

Now, let's instead take that $123,333 and put it into an IRA or 401K that lowers your tax liability (you wouldn't invest the money reserved for the church donation).

$123,333 x .25
=$30,833 in saved tax liability

Add that tax savings to the original amount of money you earned.

$137,036+$30,833
=$167,869

Then you have to add that auto insurance quote for seven years, which was around $12,600, but don't forget, that money also had to be taxed and tithed before you spent it. To do that, you would divide by .75 and then .90 like we did before. That gives you $18,666. Now you can add that to the previous total we just calculated.

$167,869+$18,666
=$186,535

If that's not enough to convince us not to buy the car, on top of all that, let's assume your IRA returns a modest 6 percent, 7 percent, or even a 10 percent compounding gain per year. Additionally, you take your tax savings and insurance savings and invest it somewhere that gets a 6 percent, 7 percent, or 10 percent return as well.

Invest $10,000 initially, which would've been the down payment for a Tesla. Then, for seven years, put $2,101 per month (car payment, insurance, and tax savings) into that investment account.

That gives you the true cost, or in other words, the opportunity cost over seven years of buying that beautiful car:

$226,661 (6 percent return)
$234,242 (7 percent return)
$258,677 (10 percent return)

Wow, I dodged that bullet! I guess the title of this chapter should've been, "the time I almost lost over $200k on a car but chose to only lose $1,000."

But wait, there's more! The plot thickens: stop adding that $2,101/month after those seven years, and let the money just sit there for another twenty years with those moderate returns. You now have your true cost of that car over twenty-seven years:

$726,932 (6 percent return)
$906,442 (7 percent return)
$1,740,249 (10 percent return)

What an insane opportunity cost! This internal financial tug of war and mental and emotional angst and turmoil was literally a million-dollar decision for me. Albert Einstein said, "Compound interest is the eighth wonder of the world. He who understands it, earns it . . . he who doesn't . . . pays it." Between now and when I'm fifty-three years old, the difference between having an extra $1.7 million dollars to my name or not could simply be in the purchase of one beautiful vehicle now or keeping the dumb little Smart Car that I bought used for $10,000 cash. I want to reiterate this quote from Jim Rohn: "An immediate reward for lack of discipline is a fun day at the beach . . . a future reward of discipline is owning the beach. For most, we choose today's pleasure over tomorrow's fortune." Is giving in to a false feeling of wealth and flaunting my status today worth sacrificing real wealth in the future? What could I do with $1.7 million? I probably actually could buy a sizeable chunk of private beachfront property in paradise. Even better, I could probably keep letting it compound and accrue more wealth and then live off the interest for the rest of my life. Not buying one beautiful car is a decent retirement plan.

So, what does this have to do with making $300K in a year? Well, it's a lot easier to make money if that money brings you security, not stuff. I try to work with a distinct purpose; at this point in my life, I sometimes work for fun, toys, or the latest gadgets, but it isn't often that I indulge. I've conditioned myself to work for causes that have a lasting and deeper purpose. Most of those purposes revolve around my greatest passion: my family. My hard-earned money buys them food, shelter, safety, and security. It buys them peace and freedom. It's been said that "money can't buy happiness." Agreed, but only if you say, "*spending* money can't buy happiness." I firmly believe that *saving* money and living below your means sure does help facilitate happiness. I've been without money, and consequently, during those times, I've been money's slave. I'd rather be the one in control in that relationship. The relationship is always very bitter for those who don't understand it, but it has the potential to be very sweet when it's owned, understood, tamed, and controlled.

Now, I'm not saying that if you own a nice car, you've made the worst mistake of your life. It doesn't mean you haven't been or can't be successful. If you have indulged, depending on your circumstances, that just means that maybe you aren't doing as well as you could at saving and investing your hard-earned money. If you own an expensive car and you're under forty, I want this to make you feel a little uncomfortable; I want you to think about the opportunity cost of that purchase. The thesis of this book isn't just about how to make a ton of money in one year. The central topic explored is how to be leaps and bounds above the pack—how to not only be in the ninety-ninth percentile but also well beyond where the percentile curve goes vertical. This can also be applied to any area of life; income is just one of the easiest to quantify. These principles can be applied to wealth accumulation, family life, spirituality, romantic relationships, bowling, cooking, chess, running a charity, running marathons—whatever your passions may be. However, there are some things that are much more important to me because they help bring balance and provide peace. An example is delayed gratification in order to accumulate wealth. This idea of self-discipline and self-control isn't a popular notion. It isn't an easy lifestyle to adopt or sustain. However, the longer you delay gratification, the wealthier you become. Discipline. Patience. Longsuffering. Temperance. Humility. These are words to live by, at least while you're young and still building wealth.

Thanks, Dad, for Having an Ugly Car

After I went through this Tesla experience and realized all of this, I remembered the cars my parents had growing up. My dad drove a thirty-year-old tan Jeep CJ-7 with a faded, poop-brown hard top (I think that might be the actual technical name of the color, it couldn't be anything else). I think that would be pretty awesome to have a Jeep like that now . . . but in a different color. Regardless, that car was not cool to me when I was in junior high. I distinctly remember the *Quadratec* magazine that would come in the mail once a month; it showed all the accessories you could add to spice up your Jeep. There were tons of paint options, winches, lift kits, beefy grille guards, less-ugly tops, stereo systems that actually worked, rims that didn't look like donuts, monster-sized tires, a wide variety of "cool" shift knobs, and every single replacement part you could imagine in shiny chrome. I so badly wanted to give the whole car a makeover, change it from looking like a beater to looking like a mean, outdoor adventure-ready beast. So, when I was a young teenager, my dad let me change out the carpet from a faded and extremely dusty beige that smelled like Florida swamp water to a nice brand-new rich black that smelled like new car. We had plans to repaint it, but for some reason, the plans to paint the exterior never came to fruition; I think my dad was worried the car would look too nice.

I vividly remember the feeling of humiliation I had as I was dropped off at school. My dad always had the ugliest car. Although, my band teacher was as close second; he drove a tannish van that looked like it was part delivery van and part minivan. I hate brown cars. There was an even greater disparity when my father would park his Jeep at his clinic next to all the other doctors. I've always heard the expression, "It sticks out like a sore thumb." Well, a more understandable expression for my junior-high self would have been, "It sticks out like an old brown Jeep in a parking lot full of Porsches." A brand-new Porsche, Mercedes-Benz, Audi, or BMW can make almost any car look bad. That Jeep made *itself* look bad. It always made me feel like I was the poorest kid in school. If anyone saw me get dropped off, they probably would've tried to get me to sign up for the free lunch program.

That Jeep was just as ugly on the inside as it was on the outside. The transmission and the engine have been replaced multiple times; I got to help a couple times. Saran Wrap was used to keep the wiper fluid from spilling. I think just about every part in that car has been replaced at one time or another.

My oldest sister learned how to drive in that car, as did most of us. One of her first experiences driving that evil machine involved her completely pulling off the shift knob while in the middle of an intersection on one of the busiest roads in town. She stalled the car and immediately started bawling. She may or may not have crawled into the back seat.

The worst experience I had in that car was when my soon-to-be wife and I were riding as passengers with my dad. We were just recently engaged and had driven in a wonderful Honda Civic from California to Wyoming to visit my family in the singlewide trailer. We had to drive to another town thirty minutes away for me to give a report on my two years of missionary work. For some reason, we opted to take the Jeep instead of the Civic. We were a few blocks from our destination when we came to a stop sign; my dad pushed on the brakes to slow down. Then, without warning and to my fiancée's horror, the brake pedal went all the way to the floor, and we didn't slow down at all. With a calm, nonchalant voice, my father said, "The brakes are out." His tone made my soon-to-be wife feel like it was a common occurrence. I also think we couldn't shift out of second gear. Anyway, we coasted through multiple stop signs as my dad was pushing the brake to the floor. Talk about an adrenaline rush! I think it may have been more anxiety provoking for me than when I went skydiving.

Safety aside, the lessons I learned from that car are irreplaceable. One of the biggest virtues that I learned from my father was humility. You aren't what you drive. Your things, your stuff, your perishable junk isn't what defines your character, your integrity, your love, your mentorship, your influence, or your importance. My dad's a doctor. He could've easily gone into debt or even paid cash for just about any car he wanted. However, instead of pursuing that self-gratification, he saw his car as a tool, not a status symbol. He used the car to get to and from work. He used it to haul a flatbed trailer to pick up supplies to build a magnificent home. He used it to tow a ski-boat that was just as ugly as the Jeep, but it gave our family so many fond memories. He used that Jeep to teach his children about mechanics. Ultimately, he used it to teach us about what really matters in this life. To me, that Jeep represents hard work, quality family time, humility, thrift, independence, wisdom, sacrifice, and discipline.

Since that time, my father recently purchased a thirty-unit apartment building, of which the proceeds will completely replace his income. Had he bought fancy new cars and toys to show off to my junior-high friends, I don't think he would have been able to have the freedom and means to basically buy his retirement plan.

If you don't have a parent like that, find a mentor, someone who is well-off but strongly exhibits the attributes of humility and delayed gratification. Pick their brain and try to emulate them. Again, I just want to reiterate that it has been infinitely easier for me to work and succeed when I don't have a mountain of li-abilities constantly in the back of my mind. I don't particularly like feeling forced into a corner, pressured to make decisions based on money. I often do make choices based on money and the economics of the situation; however, decisions tend to be clearer and smarter when they don't involve a helpless desperation for another dollar. My father's ugly car helped guide me to obtaining this sense of freedom.

In an attempt to emulate that example, I now drive a Smart car. You would never guess that I not only earn more money than most people my age, but I also earn more than most people any age. If you live in my town, you may have passed me in a double yellow because you felt embarrassed or insulted to be behind me in my tiny Fisher Price golf cart of a car. Those cars may think they're cool because they look like they actually belong on the road, but I can guarantee I never lose sleep worried about a car payment.

Thanks, Dad.

16 Work Smarter, Not Harder

My wife and I often tell our four-year-old daughter, "It's not about how *hard* you work, it's about how *smart* you work." She gets frustrated when she's trying to do something, and she thinks if she uses more strength, she'll have a better chance of succeeding. We basically tell her to take a step back and assess the situation. We encourage her to find out if there's an easier way to get the desired result with less force and a smarter concentrated effort.

I grew up working commission-only. My father refused to pay us hourly for work we did around the house. He would only pay us based on the job we were doing and then assign a value to that. My experience making commission-only has continued to this day in my career. This pay structure taught me loads of knowledge about efficiency. There's only so much time in each day; if I can achieve the same results in half the time, then I will 100 percent choose that route. My per hour income has been as low as $0 an hour to as high as thousands an hour, depending on how smart I have worked.

To illustrate this idea, I'm going to use a sports analogy. I can't think of many athletes that are in better physical shape than a Rocky Balboa-caliber boxer. Boxers are notorious for jumping rope in their workouts to increase their stamina. A fascinating study about the cardiovascular health benefit of jump roping shows that ten minutes of jump roping equals thirty minutes of running. If your goal is cardiovascular health, why run at all if you can save time and jump rope? If you can achieve the same results in a third of the time, then it makes so much sense to at least add it to your workout routine. There are a number of techniques and concepts I've learned over the years that are like jump roping; they are the fast pass to achieving success in less time. I'm going to share a few of my favorites with you.

Name-Dropping

Do you remember grade-school fundraisers where they would have you sell wrapping paper, holiday decorations, chocolates, pizza, or cookie dough?

There was always a grand prize; in fifth grade, it was a scooter for first place or a boom box for second place. I won every year I participated in one of those competitions. It really wasn't that hard because I intuitively learned how to name-drop. My dad was a family doctor working at Bond Clinic in Winter Haven, Florida. There were over fifty doctors in this one building. Well, all those doctors had nurses, receptionists, and an occasional nurse practitioner. Imagine a neatly groomed twelve-year-old boy walking up to a reception desk at a doctor's office with his big blue puppy dog eyes, a holiday magazine, and a warm grin. That probably closed all my sales before they even said anything! Anyway, I would tap on the glass or ring the bell at the reception desk and start my sales pitch with, "I'm Doctor Jones' son." With those words, I was in; I built instant credibility and my visit to their office was immediately sanctioned. I vividly remember hearing the office staff chattering as they placed their orders, one would say, "Who's that?" and another would respond, "It's Doctor Jones's son . . ." It's so much easier to buy something if you know someone who the salesman knows; there's an instant connection.

On a side note, the HR department was a black hole for sales; I never had any success there. It's interesting the valuable lessons you can learn at such a young age.

During summer sales, the weeks when I was really on point and focused on name-dropping were the best weeks I ever had. I did everything I could to set up the town's most influential people with my product. I then would mention to the neighbors that their well-known neighbor had our service, and suddenly, once you say the name of someone familiar, you can instantly be friends with a stranger. There's a connection, and that breaks preoccupation when you initially meet someone.

It's easier to let your guard down for a friend of a friend and listen to what they have to say. Just like the idea of being a human billboard, this is another way to use the Jones Effect to your advantage.

Talk to the People No One Else Does

For those same fundraisers, I remember walking up to my band teacher right after he announced it and asking him if he would buy from me. The first time I did it, he looked a little shocked but then said yes. It didn't cross anyone else's mind to talk to the person who was running the fundraiser.

My older sister recently reminded me that I called her at 5:00 am trying to sell her something. I didn't think about the time difference between Florida and California—still, it was 8:00 am my time! Her husband still remembers how confused he was: "Honey, who's calling at 5:00 am?!" To which she responded, "It's my little brother Josh selling something for a school fundraiser." I sold to everyone I knew, no matter where they lived or what time it was. Most people who did those fundraisers only sold to the people who lived in their neighborhood or would send the magazine with their parent to have their parent sell it in their office. If I would've limited myself to just my dad's office, it would've been one-fiftieth of my potential sales from his work. Also, it had to be me in person; they wouldn't have gotten the same charm from my dad handing them a magazine.

In other experiences since then, I've learned to find the homes that aren't in obvious places. Homes off of busy roads are rarely talked to by door-to-door salesmen because they don't like walking on busy roads. I guess that's a positive reason to live right off the highway: fewer pesky salesmen knocking on your door! There are also homes with longer driveways that are hidden from street view, which are super intimidating for some reason. No soliciting signs on doors are seen as an invitation. You might not agree with that, but they're always happier after I knock on their door.

Door-to-Door Sniper

I would encourage door-to-door sales for everyone. However, not everyone will succeed because it's incredibly tough. I do think it might be the easiest way to make a six-figure income, though. In any sales interaction, there is a cycle that the sale naturally follows.

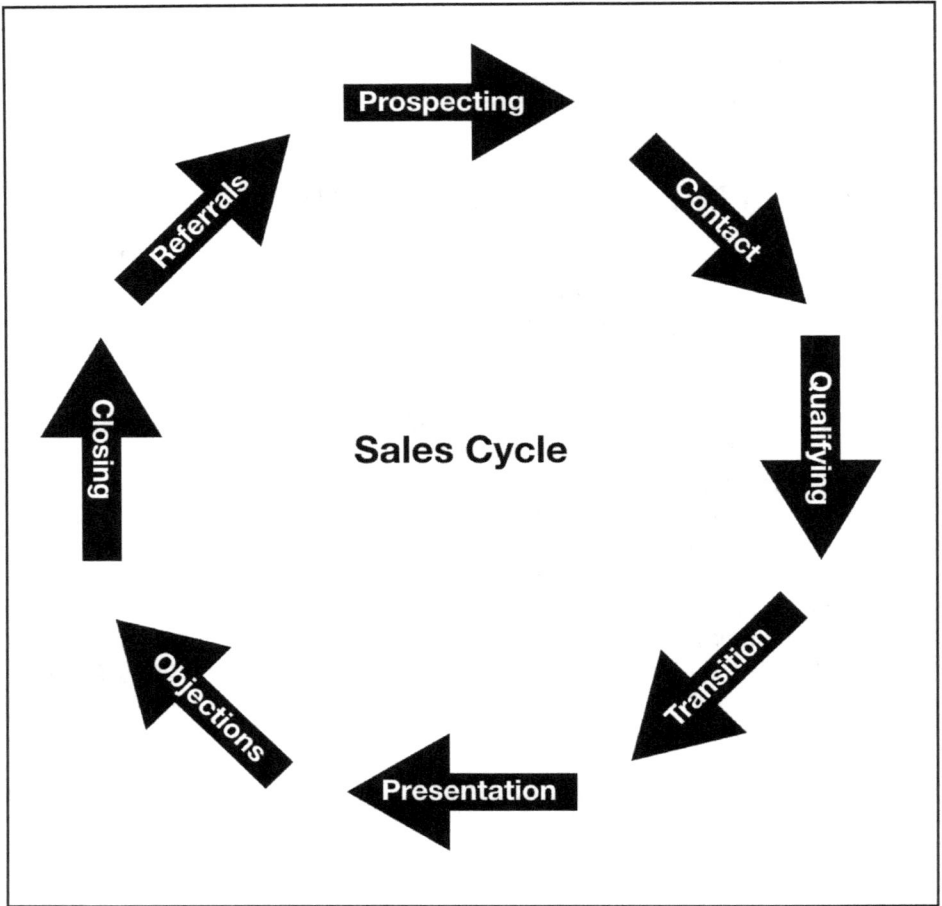

Image 17: Sales Cycle

It all starts with prospecting. When I first started selling door-to-door, I would bang on every single door on a street. I talked to 120 people before I got my first sale. I deluded myself into thinking that because I was working hard, I should be paid to match the effort. Well, I generated zero value for my company until a transaction occurred. It's super important for sales professionals to understand their conversion ratios. How many people do you have to talk to on average to get a sale? Is it 120? If it is that high, then there might be a major problem with your prospecting. I made $300K last year, and I typically only talked to one to five new people a day. Five people in a day feels like a bad day to me! That conversion ratio was possible, though, because I already put in the leg work of learning how to improve from one in 120 to my current ratio of about one in three. When I'm prospecting, it feels like I'm on a hunt. I have so many different characteristics I'm looking for. I dread getting out of my vehicle if I don't think I'm going to get a sale. I'm actually kind of lazy in that regard now. I will drive around in my car for about an hour before I'll typically knock on a door. I want every person I talk to to be as warm of a lead as they possibly can be. It takes a massive amount of emotional energy to get out of my car and talk to someone. I think that stress and anxiety is what keeps most people from selling more. Most people only have enough of that energy for half a dozen good conversations, so you have to make them count. One way to conserve emotional energy is by knocking on fewer doors and talking to fewer people. That's a recipe for failure unless you are talking to prime, qualified prospects. When you talk to the right people, talking to fewer people suddenly becomes a recipe for off-the-charts success. To help guide me in this qualification process, I created a checklist of requirements that all need to be met. This specific list is for my line of work in residential solar energy, but similar lists can be made for any industry. Before I get out of my car, I always check off the following items:

1. Good credit history. I recommend using an app that allows you to prequalify prospects' FICO score every single time; why would you ever waste time with an unqualified buyer when you know a qualified one is right around the corner?
2. Signs of life. Do everything possible to tell if the decision makers are available, whether it's at a home or an office. For direct-to-home sales, this is usually based on stereotyping people based on the vehicle they drive. Signs of life can include lights on in the home, wet tire marks leading into the garage, cars in the driveway, trash can placement, packages not picked up off the porch (usually means no one is home). Wow, I sound like a crazy ex-girlfriend.
3. Roof looks like it's in good shape.
4. Roof looks like it has enough space.
5. Roof looks like it gets enough sun exposure (using Google maps on my iPad to assess).
6. Getting pickier, I ask myself if they have visibility to my existing customers' homes. This is preferred so I can reference or "name drop" the neighbors.
7. Even more preferable is if they can see one of my company's utility trucks, as this establishes immediate credibility and legitimacy. The number-one reason someone buys my product is that they know someone else who has already purchased my product.

As I've said before, every product is different. There are different requirements for a buyer to be considered qualified; this list is some of mine that I use in my hunt for a perfect door to knock. When all those things line up, it feels like the stars have aligned and something magical is about to happen, and about a third of the time, something awesome does happen. The point is, I very carefully target my customers with pinpoint accuracy, and in so doing, I set up the sales cycle with a solid foundation. From there, I basically just need an awesome presentation and the ability to answer questions clearly, and it's a done deal.

Thinning the Funnel

Another way to look at the sales cycle is to think of it as a funnel:

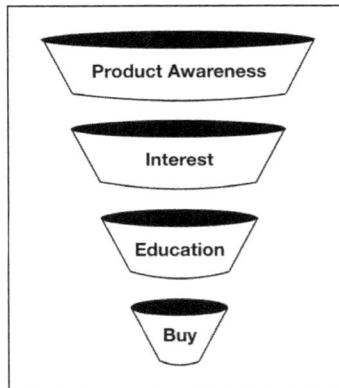

Image 18: Funnel

You start out by inputting customers, doors knocked, calls made, and people talked to. If you don't have a solid input of customers from the beginning, then you'll have a huge drop off with each subsequent level of your funnel. The worse I was at finding good quality potential customers in the first step, the wider my funnel was. Basically, what I used to do is throw every single house and person into the funnel and pray that some would stay through the process. It felt like throwing mud at a wall and then hoping that some would stick. I was working way harder than I am now, but I had to start working smarter to have my job be sustainable and to successfully make a living. I had to make that funnel thinner; otherwise, all my physical, mental, and that especially important emotional energy would be completely drained by the end of each day.

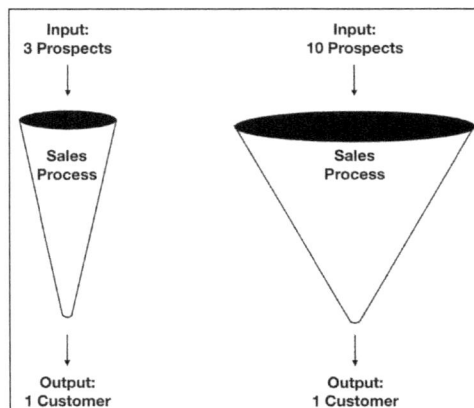

Image 19: Wide and Narrow Funnels

There are so many things that can be done to thin a sales funnel. The biggest way to add more stickiness to your clientele is to network through existing customers. Word of mouth! Referrals have a significantly smaller chance of falling through the cracks. How do you get more referrals and word of mouth? Treat your customers better than gold. Go out of your way to make them feel special. Don't ever intentionally screw anyone over, and try the best you can to not accidentally screw them over either. Be honest. Word of mouth travels negatively if you're stiffing people. Be fun, be happy, be someone who they would be confident to send their friends to. Don't make people uncomfortable. Don't ever pressure people into buying something they don't want. I have a reputation for being extremely low pressure and being super easy-going. If someone thinks you're going to make their friends uncomfortable, then they'll only send you to the people they don't like! This year, I sent out Christmas cards to about fifty of my customers. I got two referrals sent to me within a couple weeks of sending those out. I invite people into my life; I share with them and consequently, they share with me.

My goal is to try to turn every customer into two new customers. One new customer should come from a referral, the other should be one of the neighbors who sees that we worked together. This is an example of an indirect referral. A direct referral is when your customer calls you and says to go call or visit this person, or they give your information to someone who subsequently contacts you. An indirect referral is when you can basically speak through your customer; name-dropping falls into that category.

Every single one of the techniques in this chapter is an example of how the sales funnel can be thinned. This chapter will teach you how to lower the percentage of customers that fall through the cracks and ultimately don't buy your product or service.

Expectations

Setting proper expectations lowers attrition. Customer attrition is defined as a loss of customers through the sales process; it's the technical term for how thin of a sales "funnel" you have. It is a measure of how well you manage and take care of your customers. Lowering attrition is a constant topic in our sales organization. There are techniques taught and processes changed with the sole purpose of decreasing that percentage of customers who drop off somewhere in the process before they're fully committed. Millions of dollars are wasted in every organization when money is spent trying to acquire new customers but no revenue is brought in. A sales rep with 50 percent attrition is worth way more than a rep with equal revenue but 25 percent attrition. Why? Bottom-line profit is the most important number for a business. So much money is wasted on customer acquisition when you have sales reps who don't take care of their customers as well as they could. The wider your funnel, the lower your value per dollar of revenue generated.

The best advice I received was early on in my training. I spent a week shadowing one of the best salesman I've ever met, Bryce Jones. I lived with him for two weeks, and during that time, I absorbed a wealth of knowledge from observing his interactions with customers. He told me that one of the most important ways to get customers to move forward is to set clear expectations from the very beginning. If you promise or say you expect twenty solar panels but end up only being able to deliver eight, then you're in trouble and you probably won't close the deal. However, if the customer expects eight and they get twenty, then they're ecstatic. For this reason, I'm extremely thorough on my first visit with every customer. I want to make sure I establish expectations that are completely reasonable and likely to be achievable.

Another thing I do to manage expectations is when I set appointments, I always give myself a thirty-minute arrival window. For example, I word for word will tell a 4:00 customer, "I will be there between 4:00–4:30, depending on my previous appointments." I try to be there as close to 4:00 as possible, but what if I'm running thirty minutes late? It's better for them to expect 4:00–4:30 and you get there "on time" at 4:30 vs. the expectation that you arrive at 4:00 sharp and you end up arriving thirty minutes "late." I wish our 9:30 am Sunday morning church services had that same arrival window; my wife would probably be on time 95 percent of the time if she had that half-hour buffer! Life happens, traffic happens, appointments go long, customers have more questions than anticipated, bathroom breaks slow things down, children hide car keys and wallets, car batteries die, tires go flat, you sometimes run out of gas on the highway in your Smart Car, alarms go off late, the snooze button occasionally wins the first battle of the day—again, life happens. That thirty-minute buffer gives me another ounce of wiggle room; we can all use a little more forgiveness.

Along with that, at every single appointment, I say, "I'm going to send you copies of everything I just went over, so you're going to get four to five emails from me right now." There's nothing worse than a customer getting an email they weren't expecting that says, "Attached are copies of your digitally signed document." If they're surprised by that, they may feel obligated to read through every single detail of the agreement right then. I've seen this happen on multiple occasions. They get overwhelmed by the fine print that only a lawyer would fully understand. Next, they get buyer's remorse and cancel their next appointment because they misinterpreted some of the legal wording. If I tell people that I'm sending something, then they're more relaxed; they probably never even open up the attachment, and they trust that I explained all of the relevant details to them.

It's incredibly important to identify the weak points in your industry or company. In solar energy, the chief complaint is the time that it takes to get solar panels installed and then turned on. The process can often take five to seven months from start to finish. There are outliers that take over a year. We're juggling so many different variables and entities; we have to coordinate with the local utility company, state rebate team, federal rebate team, home energy auditors, town electrical inspector, insurance company, an occasional roofer and subcontracted electricians, installers, the sales rep, a customer service rep, an operations manager, the inspection technician, our document processing team, a utility interconnection team, etc. If one or two of those groups drop the ball or are slow to complete their role in the process, that adds time. Transparency is critical—you don't lead with that, though. "Hi, my name is Josh, I'm selling solar panels that take years to turn on." NO! You have to use tact, but it's so important to be open and honest. If you don't tell your customers to expect something that has a high probability of occurrence, then they may read reviews or talk to friends who have been through the process and think you were hiding something from them. That's so absolutely critical to remember, I'm going to repeat it: if you don't tell your customers to expect something that has a high probability of occurrence, then they may read reviews or talk to friends who have been through the process and *think you were hiding something from them.* Every time I've prepared a customer for those types of reviews, they just say, "You already told me that was an issue," and it's suddenly okay because they didn't find out after I met with them. I owned up to the issue, and they then knew it was a possibility that the process could take way longer than what they initially expected. It is NOT better to ask for forgiveness than to ask for permission in this case.

The Contrarian

The best opportunities with the biggest returns are often found in doing what no one else is willing to do. For example, most of the country takes off Saturday and Sunday as their weekend to relax and get shopping and work done around the house. No one likes working weekends, it seems. People dread Saturday shifts, and when they hear that you have to work on weekends, their facial expression is usually one of disgust. With that being said, I always try to work Saturdays because it is, without question, my best chance to reach and sell to the people who wouldn't be available to meet any other day of the week. Every step of the sales cycle is easier on Saturdays. It's the day that most people reserve for making purchases. The vast majority of the world is prepped, primed, and ready to consume; they just spent the rest of the week on the other end of the sales equation, they've been working and producing. It's time for them to treat themselves!

You aren't missing much by working when everyone else has the day off—lines are longer at the grocery store, theme parks, everywhere! When I say longer, I don't just mean an extra couple minutes longer. What I mean is, when I go just about anywhere on a Monday afternoon, it's dead, but when I go on Saturday, at any time, I always wait in lines for what feels like hours. I love taking a day off other than Saturday because of how efficient everything is, including shopping.

To illustrate this point, I'm going to share a financial example. In the stock market, the perceived value, or price of a stock, fluctuates between overvalued and undervalued relative to the intrinsic value of the underlying asset or company. In the realm of stock trading, there is term called a "contrarian investor." The contrarians are the ones who start selling stocks and liquidating assets when the vast majority of the population is buying in a hurried frenzy, not wanting to miss out on potential vertical stock price gains. Sadly, what goes up usually comes down, and the overvaluation ends. Everyone still exposed to the market ends up losing tons of money, begins hating stocks, and then decides to sell everything, never wanting to touch a stock again. Meanwhile, the contrarian is quietly buying up that bargain-priced stock as the average investor is selling at a loss. If timed properly, the contrarian makes a *way* better return than the person who just buys and holds stocks through the ups and downs. There is a *massive* difference in time spent vs. return achieved. I am a contrarian salesperson; I work when no one else wants to and vacation and relax when everyone else is working. The return on time and effort is so much better when you can successfully implement and follow that principle.

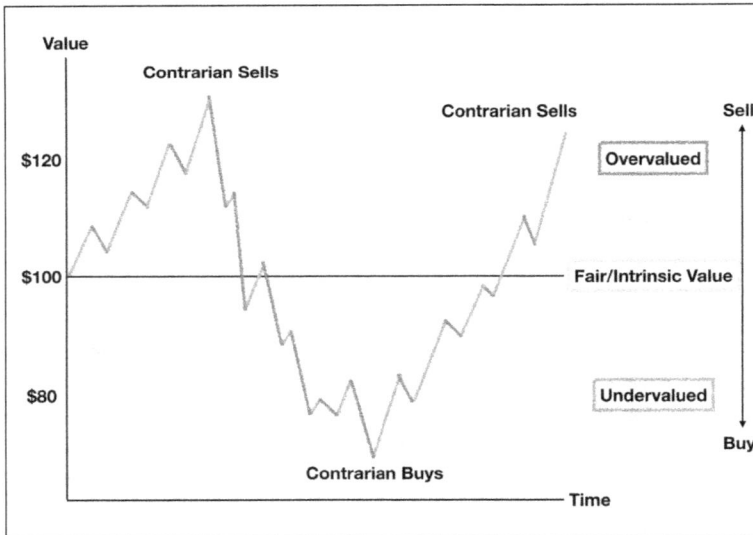

Image 20: Going against the Crowd

The professional salesperson sells on nights and Saturdays when everyone wants a break. This is just like the professional investor who bets against the general consensus. They sell their stock at the market top, when everyone mistakenly thinks the market can't go down, and buy at the market bottom, when everyone again mistakenly thinks the market will never go up again. Both the investor and the salesperson come out far ahead of the pack if they pick the right time. Choose to use your time wisely! There are only so many truly useful work hours that can be utilized consistently week in and week out.

By following this principle of always working on Saturdays and times when barely anyone else is working, I've found that I've been able to redeem a slow week. I've also seen that a good week can become a great week in a hurry. My sales production would probably be almost cut in half if I got rid of my precious Saturdays. The conversion ratio is: **1 Saturday = 3 Weekdays.** I'm positive I could take the whole week off and only work on Saturdays and make a six-figure income. That should be my retirement plan. If I did that, a lot of people would be mad at me. Wait a second, this idea is awesome! Maybe I should try it for a year and write a book about it! Would you read it?

Timing

The concept of timing reminds me of an investment philosophy I've adopted over the years: **Go all in on the despised.**

History has many examples of how timing completely makes or breaks the future. Here's an example about Nathan Rothschild, a member of one of the richest families ever:

> In the 19th century a story arose that accuses him of having used his early knowledge of victory at the Battle of Waterloo to speculate on the stock exchange and make a vast fortune.
>
> Frederic Morton relates the story thus:
>
> To the Rothschilds, [England's] chief financial agents, Waterloo brought a many million pound scoop. . . . a Rothschild agent . . . jumped into a boat at Ostend . . . Nathan Rothschild . . . let his eye fly over the lead paragraphs. A moment later he was on his way to London (beating Wellington's envoy by many hours) to tell the government that Napoleon had been crushed: but his news was not believed, because the government had just heard of the English defeat at Quatre Bras. Then he proceeded to the Stock Exchange. Another man in his position would have sunk his work into consols [bank annuities], already weak because of Quatre Bras. But this was Nathan Rothschild. He leaned against "his" pillar. He did not invest. He sold. He dumped consols. . . . Consols dropped still more. "Rothschild knows," the whisper rippled through the 'Change. "Waterloo is lost." Nathan kept on selling, . . . consols plummeted – until, a split second before it was too late, Nathan suddenly bought a giant parcel for a song. Moments afterwards the great news broke, to send consols soaring. We cannot guess the number of hopes and savings wiped out by this engineered panic.[40]

---

[40]"Nathan Mayer Rothschild," Wikipedia, Wikimedia Foundation, last modified 13 October 2017, 12:29, https://en.wikipedia.org/wiki/Nathan_Mayer_Rothschild.

That family made a tremendous fortune because they were able to position themselves at the right place at the right time, and they purchased something that everyone hated.

I made over a 50 percent return on my stock portfolio this year versus the average market return of roughly 10 percent. If I'd had more than $15,000 in there to start with, this book might've had a different title. A few years ago, I read an article on Goldsilver.com that talks about how the best opportunities to earn big ten-times or twenty-times gains are to invest in an industry or a company that is despised by everyone. If every investor in the market is bearish and the stock price has hit the floor, then there's nowhere for a price to go but up. Buy after everyone has sold. I was able to invest in a handful of companies that had their stocks completely in the dumps because the industries had been hammered. I read news articles every day, and when it seemed like even the most long-term bullish people had lost faith in a recovery for those industries, that's when I bought my stock.

Just like winning in the stock market, it's important to look for opportunities to work at the right company, in the right place, at the right time. There are certain industries poised for massive success that are unknown or even despised; getting in at the right time is like hitting a wave on a surfboard at the perfect moment. It feels glorious and the ride changes your life forever.

Delegation

Delegation is one of the most vital parts of the principle of working smarter versus working harder. If compounding interest is the eighth wonder of the world, delegation is the ninth. Delegation wields the power to create time. I'm going to show you how.

I have very little time in my life between my work, church, family, and personal hobbies. I run a team of twenty to twenty-five guys who have tons of questions, I have hundreds of customers who have tons of questions, I get dozens of emails every day that need to be answered, and I want to spend time with my wonderful wife and kids. In order for those relationships to thrive, each person in my family needs some form of affection and uninterrupted quality attention. How in the world would I find hundreds of hours to write, edit, publish, and sell a book? Delegation.

One thing I did to create more time for me to write was hire a housekeeper. That simple change made it so I could focus a little bit of extra time selling instead of cleaning, doing laundry, or washing dishes. I'll show you how in just a bit, but that little bit of extra selling time also made it so I had more time to spend with my wife and kids. I have since realized many more tasks in my life could easily be outsourced to someone else, giving me way better quality of life at home.

I decide whether to delegate a task by asking myself these four questions:

1. **How much am I worth?** Assuming a forty-hour work week over fifty-two weeks, $300K/40/52 = ~$150 an hour. Do the same calculation for yourself.
2. **What do I need done that I could possibly delegate?** I need my home cleaned.
3. **Is there someone I can hire to do this task at a lower cost than what I'm worth?** Housekeepers cost $10-$25/hour. Mine costs $15. $150>$15.
4. **Can I delegate this?** Absolutely! If your worth is greater than the cost of the delegated work, then you should almost always be able to delegate it out.

Pay really close attention to this part, this is where it gets really good:

Let me explain what I call, the **Delegation Leverage Ratio (DLR).** Let's continue with the housekeeper example. The DLR in this case is ten to one. What that means is I only have to work one hour to make what she takes ten hours to earn, or six minutes of me working is an hour of her work. I've essentially freed up, or leveraged, ten hours of workable time by delegating one hour of time already worked. The difference becomes really drastic when you look at it with more hours. If I were cleaning for 10 hours instead of working at my job, then I'm losing $1,500 of income. How much would that be if I did that every week for the whole year? $1500 x 52 = $78,000 in lost income because I didn't delegate. Hiring the housekeeper for 10 hours a week would've only cost $7,800. The difference between those two numbers is the lost profit, $70,200! That's an insane opportunity cost! In this case, having a housekeeper is actually cheaper than not having one.

The leverage this provides is invaluable. For me, cleaning doesn't feel like quality time spent with my family. One extra hour of selling buys me or allows me to leverage 10 hours of quality time at home. Or, I could spend two extra hours of time selling, which could buy me that same 10 hours of quality time at home, and it would add another $150 to my bank account.

This whole concept gets even more interesting when you factor in quality and skill level when deciding whether to delegate. Because specialists can complete tasks faster and better than someone who isn't as skilled, this is a major factor that can magnify the DLR. Let's use my barber for this example:

My barber only charges me $20, and it takes him twenty minutes, tops, to get the job done. So, his hourly cost is $60. This makes it seem like the DLR is only 150 to 60, or 2.5 to 1. However, you need to factor in how long it would actually take for me to cut my own hair and make it look as good as my barber does. I can tell you from sad experience that it takes a pretty long time, maybe two hours, and even then, it still doesn't look as good as what my barber can do in his sleep.

But let's still use that two hours for this example. Taking that much time to cut my hair is worth $300 of me selling. Because it would take me six times longer to cut my own hair, the DLR is multiplied by 6, making the DLR 15 to 1. My barber can always do the task better and more efficiently than I can. In order for me to be able to cost effectively cut my own hair, I have to be able to do it in less than 1.33 minutes. If I can't do that, then I have to go to the barber.

If the DLR is greater than 1 to 1, then it's almost always a slam-dunk, no-brainer decision to delegate it out.

I've calculated the DLR, and consequently, I tend to delegate for housekeeping, lawn care, snow plowing, haircuts, car washing, oil changes, tax prep, and grocery shopping. (If you've never had your groceries delivered, it's heaven; the time it takes me to go shopping is worth between $100–$200 and so I dread having to do it myself. If I delegate it, then it only costs $5–$15 extra to have someone else do everything for me.) I'm specialized in what I do; my time is best spent doing what I do best. In economics, this idea is called a comparative advantage. It explains why trade makes sense and can be extremely profitable for both sides. In 1808, Robert Torrens gave a macro example explaining the principle of comparative advantage:

> [I]f I wish to know the extent of the advantage, which arises to England, from her giving France a hundred pounds of broad cloth, in exchange for a hundred pounds of lace, I take the quantity of lace which she has acquired by this transaction, and compare it with the quantity which she might, at the same expense of labour and capital, have acquired by manufacturing it at home. The lace that remains, beyond what the labour and capital employed on the cloth, might have fabricated at home, is the amount of the advantage which England derives from the exchange.[41]

So, this means my trade with the barber makes me $280 every time I go there ($300 of my time saved minus $20 for his time). This economic principle of comparative advantage needs to be internalized and applied to our daily lives. I've done it and it's freed up so much time! Just like this example with France and England, it makes the most sense for me to trade with my CPA, my barber, my housekeeper, etc. By so doing, it has freed up more of my time so I can focus on my specialties and passions, which are selling, managing, writing, and being a dad. As I said before, any DLR greater than one makes sense to delegate, but the higher the DLR, the more requisite it becomes to hand the reigns over to someone else.

In order to write a book, I needed to create twenty to thirty extra hours per week for a few months. However, I didn't want to sacrifice income. I also didn't need a housekeeper for twenty to thirty hours each week; my kids can be messy but not

---

[41]Robert Torrens, "The Economists Refuted," in *The Economists Refuted and Other Early Economic Writings*, ed. P. Groenewegen (New York: Kelley, 1984), 37.

that messy! So, how else did I delegate to free up enough time to write a book? Right when I started writing this book, I coincidentally hired someone to do the most time-consuming part of my job, which is finding new potential customers. I ended up increasing my performance to have the best month of my career thus far, and I worked for fewer hours than I previously did to achieve those results. I got this idea from some of my top-performing coworkers. As I've said before, I'm surrounded by other people in my company who have done and who do way more than I do.

One rep in our company has, in five years, done what will, at my current pace, take me ten years to accomplish. In that time, he's sold more than 1,000 separate solar energy systems that have been installed on people's homes. This comes out to more than six megawatts of residential solar energy sold by one person, which is insane! How did he do it? You guessed it: he did it through delegation. His specialty is finding new prospective customers better than anyone else. Rather than continuing with the customer and guiding them to the point of installation of their system, he very frequently just generates initial interest and sets an appointment for an evaluation. Then he has someone else takes care of the client from that point on. Similarly, many of the top people in my company have delegated fundamental parts of their job to someone else who can achieve the same results, but for a cheaper price. The bigger the DLR, the bigger the profits. Had I not delegated that task, I couldn't have created the hundreds of hours needed to write down and share these ideas that have enhanced and changed my life forever.

One last thought on this topic: you need to be careful. You don't want to be *that* guy or girl that no one likes because all you care about is your specialty and analyzing the opportunity cost of every situation.

It takes a leap of faith to spend the money to delegate. The math works out, you will be better off economically, and you won't fight with your spouse as much because your house will be clean. Just trust me and do it! Delegate everything you can and focus on your specialty.

Focus on the Most Important

I was recently interviewing a super sharp potential recruit for my sales team. He told me a story that will forever be ingrained in my mind. He said that when he was in nursing school, on the first day of one of his courses, the professor made the class aware of a big project that was expected to take up a ridiculous amount of time. The professor said it should take thirty to forty hours to complete and stressed how important it was to complete the project. The vast majority of the students in the class were freaking out about that big project, and they spent most of the first month or so working to complete it. That project happened to be due around the same time as the first exam of the semester. Just about every member of the class lost focus on the first exam because they were distracted by the big forty-hour project; they focused the majority of their efforts on getting a good grade on that project instead of studying for the exam. The project was only worth a measly 5 percent of the course grade, while the exam was worth a whopping 20 percent of their grade.

The guy I was interviewing told me, "It's not about how hard you work, it's about how smart you work." He said he spent the first month studying exclusively and prepping for the exam and basically just threw his project together the day before it was due. His thought was this: "If I get a 50 percent and flunk this project, I'm only losing 2.5 percent of my grade, but if I get a 50 percent and fail the exam, then I'll lose 10 percent and drop a whole letter grade!" Most of the class failed the exam, and he managed to earn the highest grade in the class. He could've skipped the big project altogether and been better off than the majority of the class.

Weight is assigned to different projects and tests in school. The focus should be directed toward the most heavily weighted tasks. Likewise, life and work have different weights naturally assigned to different tasks. If you waste time letting yourself be consumed by the lowest weighted tasks, it will feel like you can't gain any traction. It will feel like trying to drive a car forward while the tires are spinning on ice.

I've seen this happen countless times, where my reps are caught up with the unimportant, menial details that add no marginal value. They think they're being productive, but they're not. As a society, we have expressions like, "beating a dead horse" for a reason. Focusing on the unimportant and the trivial feels like beating a dead horse. I always stress to my reps that high levels of volume fix most of those issues. Every person in the world is not qualified for your product, but it's so easy to get caught up on trying to get everyone you've ever spoken with to buy your product. Don't do it! You have to maintain a constant focus on always building a new client base. There has to be a balance there, but higher volumes of customers usually cure the pain from the small day-to-day hang ups we all encounter with the most problematic customers. I've heard numerous times from various sources about a ninety-ten rule. I can attest to the truth of it from my years of sales experience. The rule says that 90 percent of your problems and 90 percent of your time is spent with only 10 percent of your customers. Why not focus your energy on creating ten new customers rather than trying to get that one person to buy who is fighting against you or slow to adopt your way of thinking?

Let me be clear: I'm not advocating poor customer service. On the contrary, I'm advocating being selective and thoughtful in choosing whom you want to offer your product or service. After you get those 90 percent of good easy-going customers, provide them with the best service you possibly can. Don't let that 10 percent take up 90 percent of your time, and you'll have way more time than anyone else doing the same job. Just like delegation, you create way more time by focusing on the most important tasks. You need to prioritize based on what puts money in your pocket. Don't deceive yourself into thinking you're being productive by doing busywork. You have to look at the marginal value of every task you do and avoid the unnecessarily complex tasks that, in reality, never *have* to be completed. You have to ask yourself if the task you're working on is even necessary or if there's something else that would be more productive. What if your company is telling you that you have to complete an HR training? Pssh, who cares? Just skip it! Just kidding . . . sort of.

Work smarter, not harder.

Just Kidding, You Still Have to Work Harder

I want to quit my job and just give up at least once a month. It's tough, grueling, miserable work at times. I sometimes get the feeling that I just want to live in a cave and never talk to another human being again. I start moping and throwing a pity party, thinking "I have the worst life in the world." I continue with the negative self-talk, thinking everyone in the world hates me and my product. I even turn a little paranoid, thinking everyone in the world is out to get me. I ask myself in despair if anyone will ever buy anything from me again. Overwhelmed, the internal dialogue finally comes to question my whole career choice, and I, almost longingly, wonder "Why do I do this job?"

You know what resolves those feelings?

Work.

When I haven't had those feelings for a while, I realize that I'm probably not working hard enough. While in the middle of that helplessness, I've called my wife countless times to tell her that I'm giving up for the day and maybe indefinitely. I tell her how frustrated I am and that I don't know if I even like my job anymore. As I'm talking to her, I almost always seem to remember a potential customer or a referral I should stop by and visit. I tell my wife that I'll call her back after I make that visit. An hour or two later, I call her with happiness in my voice, loving life, recharged, and ready for another week of grinding toward success.

While serving my two-year mission, there was a quote that we recited regularly; it was by the former Secretary of Agriculture and President of The Church of Jesus Christ of Latter-Day Saints, Ezra Taft Benson:

> I have often said that one of the greatest secrets of missionary work is work! If a missionary works, he will get the Spirit; if he gets the Spirit, he will teach by the Spirit; and if he teaches by the Spirit, he will touch the

hearts of the people and he will be happy. Work, work, work—there is no satisfactory substitute, especially in missionary work.[42]

This principle applies to any worthy profession. If you're progressively realizing those dreams and ambitions that bring meaning to life and improving the world around you, then increasing the intensity of that work will yield success. That success yields a satisfaction that cannot be replaced by anything else. It may seem counterintuitive, but when the work gets tough and it seems like you should stop or take a break or go easy, don't do it. Instead, double down on the intensity, get your second wind, and head toward the challenge you fear. When driving in icy conditions, there's a technique called "turning into the slide." If your car starts to slide to the *right* and you're about to crash into a telephone pole, your kneejerk reaction is probably to turn *left*. That's not what you do, you should turn the wheel in the direction you're sliding. This helps the car gain traction and allows you regain control. Likewise, we need to turn toward challenges that seem dangerous in order to gain control. Turn toward hard work, and I guarantee it will increase your control over the situation and life in general.

Another example of a similarly counterintuitive situation is what to do if a certain type of bear attacks you. To survive a bear attack, you first need to know what kind of bear you're dealing with. If it's a brown bear, then you're supposed to play dead. Once you stop moving, the bear will supposedly stop attacking. However, if you're dealing with a black bear, the instructions are 100 percent opposite. "If you're attacked, your best defense is to fight back with everything you've got; punch it, kick it, do everything you can to get that animal off you."[43] Black bears will often try to bluff; however, if you stand your ground and then fight, then they'll usually back off.

Although, if I saw any type of bear, I wouldn't think, "Hmm, is that a brown bear or a black bear?" I would think, "Holy crap, that's a flipping bear!" and I would want to immediately sprint the opposite direction.

Work is not a brown bear. Don't play dead; it won't leave, and you won't defeat it by running away either. It will always catch and maul you if you run away like a little scaredy-cat. Work is a big, hairy, gnarly black bear. To defeat work, you have to attack it, punch it in the nose, kick it in the groin, elbow it the ribs, bite it wherever you can, and wrestle that beast to the ground. If you do that, I promise, you'll win.

Now, don't go intentionally picking fights with bears; we haven't even talked about grizzlies. You'll probably lose, no matter what, if it's a Grizzly. Mother-in-laws are grizzlies, but I digress—that's another topic for another book.

---

[42]President Ezra Taft Benson, "Keys to Successful Member-Missionary Work" (speech, Provo, Utah, September 1990), The Church of Jesus Christ of Latter-Day Saints: Ensign, https://www.lds.org/ensign/1990/09/keys-to-successful-member-missionary-work?lang=eng.

[43]Rheana Murray, "How to Survive a Bear Attack," ABC News, ABC News Internet Ventures, accessed 17 October 2017, https://abcnews.go.com/US/survive-bear-attack/story?id=23317682.

Mark Twain said, "Eat a live frog first thing in the morning and nothing worse will happen to you the rest of the day." I bet if you started seeing massive success from eating a frog every morning, you would start to crave it. In the case of work, you have to step out of your comfort zone, do the unnatural, stay out longer than you want to, knock a few doors after dark, try cold calling a client after 9 pm—I've done it multiple times. It's super weird and scary, but I've experienced an incredible level of success by doing things that I didn't really want to. No one wants to put in the amount work that I have. However, I can tell you that it's pretty fantastic having a housekeeper do my laundry and dishes for me. It's also pretty awesome being able to go on vacation whenever and wherever I want to. And it has been truly life-changing owning a home where my family can be happy, healthy, and safe. The feeling is so liberating, being free of burdensome debt and having savings for a rainy day. I love my life. I've come to embrace hard work, and now I absolutely love it because it rewards me mentally, emotionally, spiritually, physically, and financially. Will you embrace it too?

THE END

Epilogue:

Let's briefly return to that income percentile curve. I want to remind you of the significance of this chart. If I were thirty-six, this wouldn't have been nearly as impressive because the ninety-ninth percentile starts at $300,000.

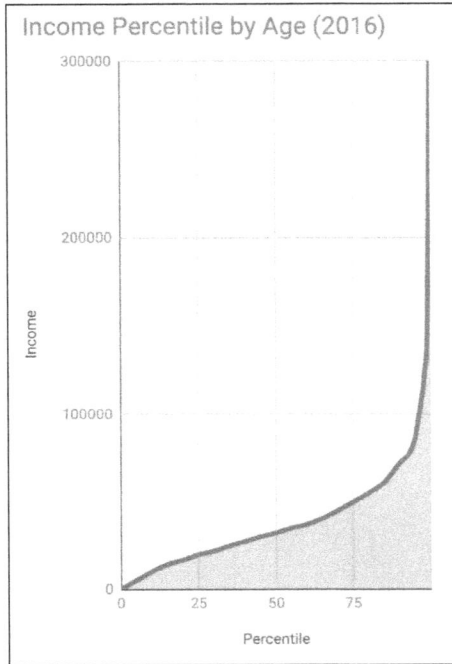

Image 21: Income

I mentioned earlier the first five elements of success from *The Millionaire Mind*. I want to remind you of those principles. I also want to add and draw your attention to number 27, which wasn't included in the list earlier in this book:

    1. Integrity
    2. Discipline
    3. Social Skills
    4. Supportive Spouse
    5. Hard Work
    . . .
    27. Luck

The millionaires surveyed for that research ranked luck very low as a factor that they believed contributed to their success. The top five on that list are all controllable, whereas luck is an abstract, intangible notion that I don't believe really exists. It's a way for explaining things you don't understand. Luck is used as an excuse for both success and failure. It's so important to accept reality and to own up to your current level of success or failure. Building wealth and earning a high income isn't supported by luck. Those who believe that they have no control over their future are in denial. Luck is an illusion that deceives the masses. The idea of luck inspires complacency and concession. I firmly believe that as humans, we are in charge of our fate because we control our daily attitudes and actions. The vast majority of people fall within a mindset of believing we are victims of life rather than masters of our destiny. Breaking free from that mindset is the first step to leaving the group comprised of the bottom 99 percent of income earners. This book is evidence that luck isn't a major factor in success. This book shows that there is a science, an extremely tough learning process that includes failing forward in order to reach the top.

I've found so much fulfillment in setting and achieving these huge income goals. It's such a rough path, but it's worth it. I want every person reading this book to be able to find that same satisfaction in life that I've found, but I want you to find it in your own unique way. It might not be income you seek, but whatever you do, figure out how to do it better than everyone else. Raise your standards and self-expectations. Don't be average; be exceptional, be the top, the best, win first place, be an icon, a role-model, a champion, the greatest.

If you've ever thought of writing a book, I highly recommend it. There's no reason not to. The title of this book is *$300K @ 26*. As I was winding down on new content, I noticed that it just so happens that when you do a word count on this book, it adds up to a little more than 300,000 characters long. I spent months thinking, pondering, and pushing keys on my laptop hundreds of thousands of times in order to put these thoughts together, not knowing if I would sell a single copy. I repeatedly thought, "Would anyone really buy *my* thoughts?" In the midst of these thoughts, I had the chance to visit Mark Twain's home in Hartford, Connecticut. It was such an enchanting place; it felt like a family who truly enjoyed life once lived there. He attributed much of the passion and creativity to create his masterpieces to the energy he received from that edifice; the home felt almost alive. Engraved in gold letters on one of the walls in the visitor center was one of his quotes: "Books are the liberated spirits of men." I really understood what he meant because of my experience writing this book. It feels as if I've taken a portion of my spirit and exposed it to the world and have hoped people will buy it and learn from it. What a scary leap of faith!

I feel like overcoming the feat of putting together the 300,000 characters in this book was an even bigger achievement and personal growth opportunity than earning $300,000. As I look at how my character has evolved throughout the process, I'm absolutely astounded. I've read so many self-help books and been impacted by the wisdom and courage of others. But even more powerful has been my process of becoming vulnerable, opening up, exposing, and sharing my thoughts and feelings while creating my own personal development book. I've reinforced in myself the core beliefs and values that I hold dear to me. I've grown tremendously through this experience of reflecting on the past. I've recognized that positive results come from the hard work, which in the moment, can feel so negative. I find so much joy in that bittersweet process of achieving success. I acknowledge that my philosophies and paradigms aren't even close to perfect. My pride will be a constant life battle. Evolution, adaptation, and course correction will be necessary every day of my future in order to achieve bigger goals and realize my full potential.

Einstein said, "Once you stop learning, you start dying." I plan to pursue education and self-actualization for the rest of my life. There's always something new to learn from everyone that may happen to find their way into your life. It's important to look for the lesson in every encounter.

As a senior in college, I decided to accept the invitation to join the Phi Beta Kappa Society, or PBK. PBK is considered to be one of the most prestigious academic societies in America. The name is an acronym for Φιλοσοφία Βίου Κυβερνήτης, which translates to: "Love of learning is the guide of life." My grandfather was also inducted as a member decades ago, and he was one of the most intelligent, knowledge-seeking scholars I've ever known. I remember how proud he was that his grandson had been selected for the same society. My grandpa Jack truly exemplified the meaning of PBK. I strive to follow that example each day to learn and apply something new.

I promise you that as you do the same, your life will be full of greater meaning, and you will achieve levels of success that are off the charts. Higher income may be your goal, or perhaps it's to be the best parent or the best spouse you can be. Maybe you want to be off the charts as a musician or a journalist. Whatever that dream may be, remember, income is just one gauge of success; true success is gradually reaching for and fulfilling your purest dreams and ambitions. If you focus on success first, the money will come as a result. In the end, though, the money will mean nothing; I would never trade my wife and three angelic daughters for any amount of money. Never. If you lose all your material possessions, those can be rebuilt and replaced. Forget all the temporal noise, vicissitudes, and distractions; ultimately, that will all disappear. Realize greatness by seeking the eternal treasures that life has to offer. With knowledge, I come to know myself; through self-improvement, I find myself.

Bibliography

Achor, Shawn. *The Happiness Advantage: The Seven Principles of Positive Psychology That Fuel Success and Performance at Work*. New York: Crown Business, 2010.

Bates, Katharine Lee and Samuel A. Ward. "America the Beautiful." 1911.

Benson, President Ezra Taft. "Keys to Successful Member-Missionary Work." Speech. Provo, Utah. September 1990. The Church of Jesus Christ of Latter-Day Saints: Ensign. https://www.lds.org/ensign/1990/09/keys-to-successful-member-missionary-work?lang=eng.

Bois, Jon. "Home Advantage in Sports: A Scientific Study of How Much It Affects Winning." SBNATION. Vox Media. Infographic. Accessed 17 October 2017. https://www.sbnation.com/2011/1/19/1940438/home-field-advantage-sports-stats-data.

BrightLocal Ltd. "Local Consumer Review Survey. BrightLocal. Accessed 17 October 2017. https://www.brightlocal.com/learn/local-consumer-review-survey/.

Cardone, Grant. *Be Obsessed or Be Average*. New York: Penguin Random House, 2016.

CUtoday. "CFOs Told They Can Still Worry. But Real Benefit Is in Happiness." CUtoday.info. Accessed 17 October 2017. https://www.cutoday.info/THE-feature/CFOs-Told-They-Can-Still-Worry-But-Real-Benefit-is-in-Happiness.

Dr. Jean-Paul Rodrigue, Dept. of Global Studies & Geography, Hofstra University. "Stages in a Bubble." The Geography of Transport Systems. https://transportgeography.org/?page_id=9035.

Frost, Robert. "The Road Not Taken." *Mountain Interval*.

Hales, Elder Robert D.. "Becoming Provident Providers Temporally and Spiritually." Speech. Salt Lake City, Utah. April 2009. The Church of Jesus Christ of Latter-Day Saints: General Conference. https://www.lds.org/general-conference/2009/04/becoming-provident-providers-temporally-and-spiritually?lang=eng.

Jobs, Steve. "'You've got to find what you love.' Jobs says." Speech. Stanford University. June 12, 2005. Stanford News. http://news.stanford.edu/2005/06/14/jobs-061505/.

Kane, Libby. "What Rich People Have Next to Their Beds." Accessed October 16, 2017. http://www.businessinsider.com/rich-people-read-self-improvement-books-2014-6.

Kevin-Mikhail Mansour Singarayar, BurningBoats. "About BurningBoats.com." Accessed 17 October 2017. http://burningboats.com/about-burningboatscom/.

Linklater, Richard, dir. *School of Rock*. 2003.

Melendez, Bill dir. "It's the Great Pumpkin. Charlie Brown." Written by Charles M. Schulz. aired October 27, 1966. on CBS.

Murray, Rheana. "How to Survive a Bear Attack." ABC News. ABC News Internet Ventures. Accessed 17 October 2017. https://abcnews.go.com/US/survive-bear-attack/story?id=23317682.

Nightingale, Earl. "Success: A Worthy Destination." Nightingale. Nightingale-Conant Corporation. Accessed 17 October 2017. http://www.nightingale.com/articles/success-a-worthy-destination/.

Nightingale, Earl. "The Strangest Secret Article." Nightingale Conant. Nightingale-Conant Corporation. http://www.nightingale.com/articles/the-strangest-secret/.

PayScale, Inc. "Chemist Salary." PayScale. Accessed 17 October 2017. https://www.payscale.com/research/US/Job=Chemist/Salary.

President & Fellows of Harvard College. "Clayton Christensen's "How Will You Measure Your Life?" Working Knowledge (blog). Harvard Business School. May 9, 2012. https://hbswk.hbs.edu/item/clayton-christensens-how-will-you-measure-your-life.

Rohn, John. *The Power of Ambition*. Narrated by John Rohn. Nightingale-Conant Corporation, 1994.

Torrens, Robert. "The Economists Refuted." in *The Economists Refuted and Other Early Economic Writings*. Edited by P. Groenewegen (New York: Kelley. 1984).

Tracy, Brian. "Setting Goals and Objectives: 5 Myths." Brian Tracy International. Accessed 17 October 2017. https://www.briantracy.com/blog/general/setting-goals-and-objectives-5-myths/.

Western. Dan. "34 Best Zig Ziglar Quotes on Leadership." Wealthy Gorilla. https://wealthygorilla.com/28-best-zig-ziglar-quotes-leadership/.

Wikimedia Foundation. "Ad astra (phrase)." Wikipedia. Last modified August 3, 2018, 20:08. https://en.wikipedia.org/wiki/Ad_astra_(phrase).

Wikimedia Foundation. "Gigafactory 1." Wikipedia. Last modified 16 October 2017, 09:53. https://en.wikipedia.org/wiki/Gigafactory_1.

Wikimedia Foundation. "Loss Aversion." Wikipedia. Last modified 11 October 2017, 20:27. https://en.wikipedia.org/wiki/Loss_aversion.

Wikimedia Foundation. "Nathan Mayer Rothschild." Wikipedia. Last modified 13 October 2017, 12:29. https://en.wikipedia.org/wiki/Nathan_Mayer_Rothschild.

Wikimedia Foundation. "Structural Biochemistry/Enzyme/Activation energy." Wikibooks. Infographic. Last modified 4 July 2017. https://en.wikibooks.org/wiki/Structural_Biochemistry/Enzyme/Activation_energy.

Wikimedia Foundation. "The Naked Man (How I Met Your Mother)." Wikipedia. Last modified 4 May 2017, 05:01. https://en.wikipedia.org/wiki/The_Naked_Man_(How_I_Met_Your_Mother).

Wikimedia Foundation. "Two-factor theory." Wikipedia. Last modified 13 September 2017, 13:22. https://en.wikipedia.org/wiki/Two-factor_theory.

Wikimedia Foundation. "Vincent van Gogh." Wikipedia. Last modified 16 October 2017, 15:26. https://en.wikipedia.org/wiki/Vincent_van_Gogh.

In 2014, Joshua graduated cum laude from the University of Wyoming with a BA in chemistry, along with minors in Spanish and finance. He is a member of Phi Beta Kappa, the meaning of which exemplifies his character: "Love of learning is the guide of life." Joshua currently resides in Connecticut, where he works in the renewable energy sector as the CEO of Elite Energy Consulting, LLC. He has been married for seven years and has four beautiful daughters. Those five girls are the pride and joy of his life. This book is dedicated to them.

www.ingramcontent.com/pod-product-compliance
Lightning Source LLC
Chambersburg PA
CBHW060558210326
41519CB00014B/3506